River Tips

And

Tree Trunks

Notes and Reflections on Water and Wood

S. H. Semken

Ice Cube Press
North Liberty, Iowa

River Tips and Tree Trunks:
Notes and Reflections on Water and Wood
by Steven H. Semken
©1996 first edition
2 4 6 8 9 7 5 3 1

SAN 298-9085

Published by the Ice Cube Press
205 North Front Street
North Liberty, Iowa 52317-9302
Orders and comments welcome

Library of Congress Cataloging Number
96-97009

ISBN 1-888160-63-2
Manufactured in the United States of America

Lines from Barry Lopez's *Rediscovery of North American,* ©1991,
reprinted by permission of Sterling Lord Literistic, Inc.

Permission to use lines from *Becoming Native To This Place* granted
by Wes Jackson.

Permission for use of T. S. Kuhn's *Structure of Scientific Revolutions*
granted by the University of Chicago Press.

Permission to use material of T. J. J. Altizer, "Eternal Recurrence
and Kingdom of God," granted by T. J. J. Altizer.

"The Sound of Water: Part 3," was previously published in Vol. 2
No. 1 of *Sycamore Roots: New Native Americans.*

Cover painting by Andy Driscoll ©1996

Thanks to all who helped with readings and offered advice, insight, and encouragement — G. Max, Paul Steinbrecher, Denise Low, Laura, Rip, Kit, Michelle Rubin, Andy Driscoll, John Patzman, and Russ Lockhart. Thanks as well to Mr. Jack Ozegovic, who always offers honest words of support, and Dr. Mark Wilson, the man able to see light through storms.

Almost river,
sometimes tree.
Go make birch bark float.

RIVER TIPS

E VERYTHING STARTS WITH THE FLOW OF WATER WITH THE MOVEMENT OF A RIVER. WHEN first spotting a river, prepare to stand in awe. Understand that it is normal to fully anticipate greatness in water. To have an addiction to liquid flow and current.

Some rivers that I admire, I do so for their varying degrees of turquoise coloring. Subtle colorings offer a method to determine a river's depth. If reminded of a coral reef when looking at a creek or river, I become way too pleased. Clear, cold water continually wants to intoxicate my mind.

There are muddy rivers worth paying homage to as well. These occur because of torrential motion, drainage and upheaval. A good, mucky river, as some in the Midwest, when they go around bridge supports for instance, spew muddy whirls and patterns in the water, behave like bursts of flame as they go by the watchful eye. It seems that a portion of the mud gets used by birds. Surrounding most bridge supports it is easy to spot swallows flying up down and around, grabbing bugs and making mud houses attached to dirt, wood and cement. It's crossed my mind, since I never see these birds leave the confines of riverbanks, that they are able to grab invisible mud, spewed forth from the river, in mid-air, and make their homes out of the contents of mist.

A heavy spring rain or sudden snow run-off can provide extreme mud. Water rising up to produce multiple series of waves, nodes and splashes that careen up over dams and embankments, producing much, junky, root beer type foam. These sorts of things are the beginnings. With rivers at first, you look, always, with hope.

It is also worth walking along a river when it is low. The low level of water allows old glass chips, smoothed out by current, and old bottles with corks still in them to be found. I have heard stories of people finding dinosaur bones and relics of the past within the exposed shores when a river becomes low.

The concept of wild and scenic comes to mind when a river is high and full of water. The idea of a hunter-and-gatherer makes sense when walking a river during a year of drought.

Rivers so infatuate me that I even get excited when many types and large quantities of insects are rising off the water (especially if there's a fly rod in my grasp). Honestly, it is hard to remember when I ever had a poor first impression of a river. I may come to recognize problems in one quickly, but not upon first glance.[1] I look at each river for the first time hypnotized with anticipation. When someone asks me what I am doing, curious about my far-away look while gazing and speaking to water (sometimes I can be found looking at cement water fountains), I answer, "Doing a little water study is all."

MYTHS, PROPHETS AND MADNESS
The language produced from cave dwelling, from isolation, from out of a different world, is that which comes from the twist off the tip of fire.

Throughout time philosophers have been able to increase their understanding of reality by being out of

---

[1] This first glance of a river is fascinating and makes me question one aspect of highway engineering. Why do they make bridge siding now that you can't see rivers through? This eliminates an entire aspect of excitement for myself and many others I'm sure. Then again, maybe seeing the instantaneous vision of the water caused too many drivers to turn the steering wheel hard right, hoping for the promised land.

this world, tempting common knowledge. Madness can lead to enlightenment. Consider the following statement: *"Man cannot bear the full burden of reality. Consequently, only in illusion does culture flourish or even survive."* [2]

The results of obsession and madness can be much different than a mad person. Engulfed with obsession, madness becomes larger than life. Paradigms[3] are the result of positive obsessions as one integrates new ideas into a different understanding of reality. To see through shadows, to read fluently between the lines, is breaking through.

Obsession and mystery must become satisfactory and faithful partners to understand rivers. Why? Rivers don't speak or present themselves in any understandable manner. They are motions of mystery. Potions of the invisible. Thus, a caution is in line: a river can very easily drive you mad on the way to understanding. A river is the display of positive madness.

Another idea in this regard is that of a prophet. Allow a river to take on the qualities of the following idea: *"Is not a prophet one who speaks what is unsayable to others, but which, once spoken, immediately carries its own authority?"*[4]

---

[2] Idea and quotation from *Prophets of Extremity* by Allan Megill (California, 1987).

[3] My concept of the paradigm as obsessive break through is derived from the work by T. S. Kuhn's book *The Structure of Scientific Revolutions* (Chicago 2nd edition, 1970). From this book he explains the paradigm, as that which, "requires the reconstruction of prior theory and the re-evaluation of prior fact."

[4] From an essay by Thomas J. J. Altizer entitled "Eternal Recurrence and Kingdom of God," printed in *The New Nietzsche* ed. David Allison (MIT press ed., 1985).

The trick is to have confidence[5] that a river won't lead you astray. That it presents information, usually unexplainable, as it flows. This presentation of information must simply be taken for granted and not doubted. Needing certainty, but not finding it, can easily crush the human brain. Realize that making partners with a river will definitely make you crazy at some point.

If one uses the river as Nietzsche's *Zarathustra* uses the cave, one can make a vessel for paradigm work. One can begin hearing and listening with earnest to the voice of a prophet. Reap the harvest of being mad. Stare at many rivers, invite frenzy to flow into your mind!

ONE VERSUS ANOTHER

It isn't a good feeling to compare things that you have cherished with full heart at different points in life. Yet, honestly, the upper (and middle and lower for that matter) portion of the Williamson River, in the Klamath Basin of southern Oregon, makes the Kansas River, running through Lawrence, Kansas, seem what this Midwestern river has truly become: a once beautiful, but now sadly polluted and badly abused stream.

The Kansas River authorities, close to where I used to live, put up a sign, where most people go fishing regularly, that says (I paraphrase) *WARNING. EATING FISH FROM THESE WATERS MAY CAUSE SERIOUS HEALTH PROBLEMS.* Then the sign goes on to state that eating more than some absurdly small amount of

---

[5] Some may call this confidence, "faith." Alan Watts, in *The Wisdom of Insecurity* (Pantheon, 1951) says, "Faith has no preconceptions; it is a plunge into the unknown. Belief clings, but faith lets go."

fish, like 1 oz., over an equally absurd, short period of time, like three months, could be a problem. This really is a problem and not only for fishermen.

Of course, my assumption is that by the time officials admit to a problem like this, things are probably so completely out of control that you had better take cover and hide. I become seriously concerned when officials, or politicians, pronounce a problem with eating the fish out of a river, and do so casually, with no press release, simply placing a sign in the ground for legal purposes. I often wish that there would be ground breaking ceremonies for these types of events.

With the appearance of this sign one morning, while riding my bike to work, a shudder and much suspicion began to rise in me. I remembered when they sprayed "green stuff," all over the levee, the year after they cut down all the trees that were growing amongst the levee rocks in and along the river. This was the same year of the summer floods in 1993. Also the same year, when invaded by the "green stuff," that many of the animals in the neighborhood got sick. Some died. My cat nearly died and still suffers from some strange, mutilated eye sickness: detached and floating eye coloring, and of course, noticeable blindness.

This sort of behavior, the spraying of "green stuff," certainly couldn't have been healthy for the Kansas River, yet I know of no complaints that were made, even by myself, I am afraid to admit. However, I fully believe, and now act accordingly, that complaints have to be made and letters sent whenever unusual acts against nature are made. The folks getting the "green stuff" sprayed do so by pushing their opinions through the system. One has to understand the logic of social change and understand the hypocrisy of not taking a stand and drawing the line.[6]

A good (albeit extreme) example of this drawing-the-line attitude is possible within the democratic process, as described by Paul Goodman. He recommends that a person who votes simply because he or she wants to choose the lesser of two evils ought to really support, or begin a campaign based on Not Voting. In this way, your words and your actions become fully consistent with your beliefs.

I hate to think of a river poorly. It isn't good to realize problems such as those the Kansas River now has. Chemical content in the flesh of fish takes time to build up and occur. It isn't something that happened with the snap of a finger one day. You hear talk of two-headed turtles in other rivers and streams. I expect mutations like this to arise in the Kansas River shortly, if they haven't already.

The most discouraging thing about problems, like not being able to eat the fish, is that they weren't and aren't inevitable. That is, society doesn't need to travel the road of destruction. With less effort at electrical based and marketing improvements, more destruction could be avoided. Unfortunately, now that various messes exist with water, things will be slow to fix. I have a feeling

---

[6] In the reissue (1962 ed. including both the 1945 and 1962 pamphlets) of Paul Goodman's *Drawing the Line*, one can find valuable explanations of how complex it is to live a firm and consistent life. All of one's actions have an effect on the self and the world. One *must* believe this and act accordingly, by "drawing the line."

that things will get much worse before they get better. Our methods and current traditions of repair don't instill much hope.

Sometimes, though, I fear that the varieties of repair and fixing will be even worse than the destruction itself. The idea that we can easily repair our problems is highly over-rated. It is the very mind-frame that causes problems to occur with ease in the first place. The use of a repair mentality in our culture has become an excuse to approve error. We have come to believe, like faithful church goers, that being responsible is admitting that there may be problems, and that, since we can repair, we can ignore error. We are a society hoping for, and convinced that maids can pick up after us, silently and miraculously.

RETURN OF DARWIN'S BEAGLE?

I don't ordinarily think of myself as a Social Marxist, or Darwinist,[7] but consider that all living organisms are capable of adaptation; whether good or bad, this provides for both positive and negative destinies. If human sterility is in fact a rising problem (or saving symptom), think of who is then being reproduced: probably those most adapted to chemicals.

Antibiotics, like penicillin, lose their potency over time. Do we want to accept overindulgence and artificial adaptations as vehicles for change in the future?

---

[7] Although not a political Marxist, I am, to a degree, a philosophical Marxist, at least in the belief that historicism is a viable explanation of social progression. Which, I suppose, explains history as hypothetically predictable, outside of time, as linear development. People often speak of a "return" to the old ways, yet, in my opinion, the "old" ways are what have created what we have now. Why would we want to do that? I want a solution for maintaining rivers, not a temporary turning back of the cycle.

Furthermore, what if a psychological adaptation occurs as well. Perhaps the admirers of cement and hair spray will inherit the earth, while the dreamers of grizzly bears and pesticide-free soils shall perish as they are unable to adapt to the chemical balance that surrounds them.

Part of this basic Darwinistic thought frame is beyond "fixing things." However, there is a form of cure through adaptation, culminating as a new breed: what I would call the Self-Serving, Unfortunate Strong who will, but don't necessarily deserve to, inherit the earth (one could describe this group as the tyranny of the majority). That is, the survivors may be those most adapted to chemical saturation and dependency. Survivors, then, would not actually be the strong at all, but would be survivors through mere quantity and probability; making those with good intentions, literally, a lonely and extinct group.

ESCAPE ROUTES

When I was little, my friends and I threw snowballs at cars off a high ledge, and when a car would stop, we had a long, well cleared, escape route. We never got caught, and knew we wouldn't, because no one would be able to run up a snowy ledge, enter the woods and still be able to catch us. This made it easy for us to go about pegging cars with snow balls. If it hadn't been so easy to fix our potential dilemma of being caught, we wouldn't have been so calm about being destructive. At the same time, if we had gone on throwing snowballs long enough, we would have been caught and probably in a bigger heap of trouble than if we had been caught early on. Imaginary and momentary safety is not real, or healthy. How do you fix what you have no idea you'll ever need to fix?

It is important to understand, then, that all problems can't just be fixed. I understand that this is not a new idea, but at the same time, hope and effort spent in understanding how to fix problems should only be thought of as another alternative, not counted on as the reflexive, and only process to health.

To criticize hope, and cherish strong efforts at fixing, is not entirely right either. I understand that people with the hope and desire to fix are the good guys right now. However, most of the time they seem to be strangely related to the same ones who caused the problems in the first place. The problem with this is that you get nowhere when the good and the bad guy is the same. It is the now familiar situation: the unaccountable bureaucrat able to blame another, who blames another, as if no one makes decisions. Somehow, we are to believe, things just happen because that's the way things work.

The bureaucratic process can create results without pride or accountability, suggesting one of the primary problems of specialty: no one really does know what's happening. It's quite possible (and frightening) that no one is to blame for things like dioxins, fluorocarbons, oil spills, etc. That is, the worker only makes the stuff, and the shift manager only sees to it that the worker makes the stuff as fast as possible since fastness indicates a good job of management. The product created is then irrelevant to the manager in this way. The person designing the product only does so in a commercial manner, thinking of what will sell, not thinking of what they are actually selling. The owner probably knows that his company is making something, but after years of letting the product develop, he/she may not even know what's really being produced ("It's been out of my hands for years," she/he may say). Maybe this is why you hear VIP's and CEO's speak of the past and their glory days so often, because when they first started their business, they really did produce something well.

A company cleaning up its pollution is only inevitable, known ahead of time. Yet, there's a profit to be made from destruction, and most companies make little, if any real effort to clean up after themselves as they go along. Waiting, instead, for the day of the big pay-off when it comes time to clean up.[8]

This sort of thing, being made to clean up your own inevitable mess and acting noble for it, should be labeled an obvious, NO-DUH act. Are we to believe that groups and businesses, are so (un)green that they can't anticipate a mess and/or the solutions? Cleaning up your mess is a strange way to emphasize concern. Temporary insanity and selective incompetence are not ways out; the mess was already known ahead of time. I do believe this though: most people are behaving temporarily insane when they say they care about cleaning up the environment.

---

[8] It seems relevant to me that places which serve hamburgers in triple wrapped paper should be held accountable and made to clean up the waste in the streets which at one time contained their hamburgers. This may not be a legal obligation, but it would certainly be taking responsibility for the inevitable by-product of a paper wrapped product. You can't expect people to clean up after themselves. After all, there are no role models to enhance this behavior. A good source for these types of solutions can be found in Paul Hawken's book *The Ecology of Commerce*.

Like our health system, we have no concept, pay no heed about how to maintain[9] health, only how to overcome ill-health. We are also quite proficient at recognizing problems and paying people good money to monitor whether problems occur, but beyond that, not much detail is desired. So that fixing is what we're left with. Hopefully, we can locate and create maintainers at some point, like, hopefully, we can encourage people to take an interest in their home regions[10] after college and not continually squirt away to no-duh jobs in metrosettings.

As an aside, in this regard, (and an indication of a poorly maintained society) I had a friend in school who was very interested in farming. He was attending the state's agricultural school to learn more about farming. However, the last I heard he was working in some Chicago suburb doing some business stuff. This guy had a desire and talent in agriculture which, from pressures to make money and be important, he may never realize. He will miss out, as will the community, on ever experiencing a homecoming. Which is too bad, as lord knows, genuine people, with an emphasis in stewardship, are needed in the farming and land occupations these days.

This fixing thing may end up working like this. The only way to improve a slightly bad river will be to dump

---

[9] For that matter the entire concept of maintenance is a forgotten and shunned idea anymore. The rapid, gattling-gun style of new housing developments is indicative of this, especially when there are perfectly good older houses in need of restoration.

[10] Home region could be anything from the same city, to the same bio-region, or economic area.

tons of liquid drain cleaner in and make the watershed a bad enough problem that it will require fixers to finally come in and take care of the situation.

In the meantime, since this is what we are stuck with, don't knock the people acting as fixers. What will scare me is when people give up hope and simply let things be destroyed and fall to pieces. I am not confident enough to believe that humans will ever evolve to the point when we won't need fixers.

For now, maintenance shall remain an ideal, a concept scoffed at by most grown-ups, who lead immature lives anyway, needing the law to guide their bits of responsible life.[11]

Hope Continues

With all this said, the Kansas River does have good qualities (as well as other rivers like it), and I do believe it can be restored, no matter how dismal the current qualities are.

Presently a person would be lucky if he or she were able to see down into the water of this river more than a couple of inches, on a good day. Not only is the water contaminated and muddy, the river is also silting out wider and wider each year. As a result, more and more of the much-needed trees continue to fall down along the river's banks. It's hard, if you're a tree, to grow when

---

[11] In the western city I stayed in one summer the people going to the small claims court seemed a bit too gleeful, going in to be scolded by a judge. This sort of mind-frame amazes me. I interpret these actions like this: one gets attention only when one messes up, and so one must mess up because they like attention, or rather, a good angry scolding. Many people seem incapable of taking care of themselves. Wanting to break the law to feel involved in society is a fully immature manner of behaving.

the dirt is washed away. In tree philosophy, it could be understood with the following maxim: one cannot grow on water, sun, and air alone.

Sadly, it wouldn't take much visualization to come to the belief that the Kansas River serves one primary function, that of a drainage ditch (people seem perfectly content with a future of purchasing cleaned up or natural water from the store, not understanding, it seems to me, that this means their home is deathly contaminated). I would guess that if one were to closely examine the statistics and amounts of toxins, pollutants and other damaging inputs to the Kansas River the report would feel heavy and oppressively disheartening. I would further venture a bet that, technically, if the water were checked following a heavy fall rain, when most fields are bare, and cities (as they become increasingly covered in cement) incur quicker drainage, that the Kansas River really could be classified as a drainage ditch.

It's hard to see how people can side with industry, residential development, and farmers (many using loads of chemicals) and still claim to have any interest in health. Most business is simply a process of continued destruction. To have mercy, or make excuses for any obvious or covert processes of pollution, is to take the easy way out and over rationalize, using the belief system of the Holy Fixer Mentality. One would do well to make the polluters aware that their actions aren't acceptable.

The Holy Fixer Mentality is that which makes excuses for harmful behavior, knowing what it's up to, but pretends not to know (NO-DUH'ers). The agribusiness industry knows, full well, that it is exploiting the land and the environment. This doesn't mean that it will stop. Any hope to stop the current practices are sadly dependent on mostly non-resident owners and policy makers to change. Unfortunately these people are mostly ignorant, making excuses for destruction, erosion and pollution by using such phrases as "I didn't know," or "I forgot."

It is deemed, in this day and age, as safe and better to live away from your damage. To be able to easily cover your trail and flee, like when I used to throw snowballs at cars. I felt safe because I was close to an escape route. In addition, if you aren't around when the destruction occurs you can't be unaccountable because: 1) You never knew this was happening. 2) You didn't have time to check on what was happening. 3) You sold that land last year or hired a new helper this year. 4) It was fine when you owned it or will be now. All weak rationalizations that attempt to escape responsibility.

This type of behavior, once again, is that of an immature process, one that is accepted precisely because it allows one to be unaccountable, and irresponsible, and at times, promoting an attitude that looks forward to a scolding. As one of my friends says, "Our system is like this: everything would be O.K. if people would follow the rules that our parents told us to follow, except for me. I should be allowed to break the rules while everyone else follows them, since I really do know what's best."

To think of the term given a river, that of "natural resource" (a strange industrial term in its own right), inherently attempts to identify the water of a river as a potentially exhaustible item that can easily be replaced.[12] Not to accept the whole meaning of "resource" is to walk on a bridge, when told the bridge is broken. Tending, having fidelity toward "resources," is only confirming what you already claim to believe in if you accept the actual term "resource." A river, or a resource, is finite and therefore must be treated with care if you expect it to continue as long and as well as possible. That is, a river may be a finite item, and the full implications of it being treated this way are painful. It would be better if a river were called a treasure and treated as something sacred. In my opinion a mind frame based upon sacredness and treasure promotes high respect and allows for mystical manners of behavior.

The pollution of a river is not equal use, considerate, or intelligent. Not being able to swim in the Kansas River, for instance, without becoming covered in various mud-like coatings is a further, and simple, indication of things gone sour. (The cork on the bottle of society has gone dry. We have been standing upright for too long. Let us rest, on our side, in the dark, become revitalized and properly aged.)

UNFORTUNATELY THE SOCIAL RAG MUST BE
CONTINUED A TAD BIT LONGER
Perhaps acts like walking, bike riding, or river swimming are not done enough these days. I firmly believe that this is one of the major obstacles to getting things done through the system. Comparisons and arguments can

---

[12] These days the term "resource" means an item that can be used, abused, manipulated, worn-out, and supposedly replaced.

only be effective if both sides of your comparison are potentially understandable, or able to create empathy in the opposing party. To speak of swimming or biking or walking is often the trigger, when directed at a bureaucrat, or elected committee, which puts them in opposition to you, instantly. To speak in such basic terms will get you laughed at. After all, important policy makers are much beyond walking and swimming and biking, especially as parts of their everyday lives.

It becomes hard to relate natural problems to officials who are (I find officials to be a separate species) slowly turning unnatural and modern. The link between most policy makers and natural these days is that one has the right to look young forever, or rather, to retain that youthful, natural look and feel, which is, of course, petty, painful, and pathetically un-natural.[13]

You will succeed in helping a river, not if you speak of it as dear to you, but only if you speak of the river as a nonexistent entity: perhaps as something that was full of family values. Effectively argue for the river as being greater than, or equal to, apple pie, but also equal to or greater than the savings and loan fiasco. This will get you somewhere. Save the river by making it disappear.

The sad thing about the recovery of or education about environmental protection is that, as it has been said by many conservationists, most control and conservation of both land and water is indirect. It's

---

[13] Yet another symptom of the immature society: fifty-and-over men and women, obsessed with keeping their youthful appearance and potency. What these older people are really saying is, "Mommy, Daddy, look at me. I am still so cute." Of course these older people's children are the ones who are usually the substitute parents being spoken to.

mostly about controlling mankind.[14] Here then is the catch: the problems are with those who don't have any comprehension of any problems in the first place. It's like throwing yourself into a brick wall, or jumping off the Empire State Building and landing on the ground softer than a feather. The obvious and expected are no longer clear.

Nearing the End of the Social Commentary and Onwards to Wild and Undiscovered Waters

Fortunately, this is a book about rivers, not politics, and rivers give me hope. My faith in rivers and the good work of caring people tell me that the Kansas River will recover. I believe that rivers are deep inside people. Deeper than laws, farming practices, and liquid drain cleaners. I believe that water and rivers are held, favorably and as necessary, with compassion, inside the human unconsciousness.

Water will ultimately speak and control us as a species. Our natural instincts will, like a werewolf, emerge and savagely save us. This will be uncomfortable for people who have repressed the natural and cultivated an appreciation for vinyl siding. When the river inside us runs through our normally calm and so-called middle-class society, people will involuntarily lash out. Later, they will make excuses around the tea table or in the corners of the auto parts store about some strange, wild behavior that popped out of them, like the day they

---

[14] These sorts of ideas are well expressed in Robert M. McClung's book *Lost Wild America*. Try the new 1993 ed. by Linnet Books.

signed a petition to save the wetlands or, better yet, volunteered to help pick up trash along a river.

As long as this good work is repressed and unconsciously done, then it will be O.K. We'll feel satisfied and glad that we don't have to admit any sort of ownership over responsible acts, or be embarrassed when caring about conservation. After all, sociologically speaking, our culture's addiction to self and irresponsibility, such as the wish for youth[15] all the time, can only be repressed for so long. The werewolf will pop out from time to time, making it the only real hope we have to be saved.

Pockets of people, during these days of consumption, overpopulation, and immature living, are establishing Grass Roots[16] solutions. Those whom I call the New Natives of an area: people dedicating themselves to restoring where they live, in a locally specific manner. In the words of Barry Lopez, from his book entitled, *The Rediscovery of North America* (Vintage, 1992), *"If we mean to make this a true home, we have a monumental adjustment to make, and only our companions on the ship*

---

[15] I hope to avoid much more talk of things other than rivers, but this can't be avoided. I'll make it quick. Parents, if you aren't willing to give up your lives for your children, don't have them! Accept that being a parent means admitting your death; bringing new life into the world. Secondly (I apologize for basically repeating myself but can't help this youth thing), getting older, looking older is inevitable. Most of the models in advertisements are in grade school. You can't be old and look young, it's self-centered and unhealthy. It is a NO-DUH attitude.

[16] A second rate label, like "alternative," that people have accepted. When you hear the term "grass roots," even as a supporter, it feels more like a hobby, than those other things called PAC's, or lobbyist. Labels, unfortunately, are very very important in this day and age. Think of how powerful advertising is. If strong venom is plugged into the doings of grass root organizations we can make them very real though.

to look to. We must turn to each other, and sense that this is possible."

Around Lawrence, Kansas and the Kansas River, various groups will figure out ways to maintain and improve the water shed region close to themselves. I am aware of a strong, well-voiced coalition of citizens that turned back a river dredging proposal for the Kansas River with their cohesive organization during May of 1995. The result: a much more accurate interpretation of Neil Armstrong's saying, "one small step for man...."

THE KANSAS RIVER CONTINUED
Consider this, for good and for bad: bald eagles, in the last few years, have begun to return to the Kansas River banks. I saw one land on the branch of an old cottonwood, right beside one of our country's flag. I will explain a little of what this made me think. Symbolically I was overjoyed to be where the bald eagles were. To walk along the river bank and spot thirty old and young eagles is a thrill. The winter they showed up after the danger sign was placed, the one warning of contaminated fish, I felt less excited about the eagles being along the river.

This is all happening next to an outlet mall, built upon what was, even when built, a known perching ground for the bald eagles. This was bad enough. Granted there are still trees along the river, fewer each winter as the river seems to flood wider and easier each passing year, bringing down more and more cottonwoods, the very ones I have seen eagles sitting in. The location of the eagles can be quite precarious, sometimes in front of the outlet mall windows, which seems quite degrading. I am sure that for some people this makes for a cool glimpse of a big birdie. When I see an eagle I understand it as having a fully developed, complex life. An eagle is not useful only as if part of a geeky, freak-show circus. The bald eagle is a great symbol precisely because it is way beyond being a symbol.

Also, consider this. It is possible to align yourself, next to the Kansas River, on the North Lawrence side of town, for perhaps a sadly, yet true United States view. You can stand by the sign declaring the fish unfit to eat, confirming pollution; while at the same time view a bald eagle, in an old cottonwood, next to the United States flag which is hanging by the river, in the parking lot of the outlet mall. This is not the type of river image I am particularly fond of, but I do grant that it is interesting, both symbolically and realistically.

AROUND ANOTHER BEND ON THE RIVER
The sound of riffles, of rapids, or of a slow, backwards moving eddy is music beyond classification. Because I enjoy fly fishing, I often look at a river and think of where the trout may be, paying attention to rising fish and the type of insects that are moving and hatching. But I am not nearly so one-sided. I also cherish the tranquillity, flow, and silence of water, not to mention many more feelings that I can't begin to put my finger on. Within the presence of a river I lose quite a bit off the tip of my tongue.

Rivers make my mind go astray, off nix. I know I am not alone in this regard. Even my parents, normally sedate and very rational, proper-acting people, go mildly berserk around water when they get the opportunity to go snorkeling along a coral reef. I appreciate this behavior and chalk it up to that deep seed in the cave of the human psyche. The same seed that I hope will save the nation. That deep werewolf kernel, way down in the unconscious realm, where water takes control and is allowed to flow and be set free.

A FAITHFUL PARTNER/REMINDER: THE ALMOST RIVER
I have met people who, when they move, out West for example, feel frightened and insecure upon arrival: lost amongst all the open landscape and the broad variety of solitude. There is the whiz of pick-up trucks, the realization that the West isn't the land of the individual, but the space where people have been exploited by one thing after another (and have reasons to feel anger): gold, railroads, trapping, logging, skiing, espresso, tourism, the list goes on, as long as the people who have moved. To put it simply, the West isn't all that cozy and may never be a place to live for some people.

When you first get to the West, or any new place, things can seem stark. For dreamers out of the Midwest, it is a shock that they may never feel good about. A cure, for some, to get rid of these irritating feelings, can be the search for a good river. Like one of the beautiful forks of the Yuba River in Northern California, portions of the St. Croix River in Minnesota, maybe the Rogue River in Oregon, even the Upper Iowa River in Iowa. Here a person can take time to sit and think, meditate, making use of the river and its motion as an elixir, a strong medicine.[17]

A river invites. Along the Rogue River I was brought to tears, for many reasons. I had moved from Kansas to Oregon, for all the wrong reasons. I wanted a river, the Rogue, but the river told me there is more than looking and wanting. I was reminded of the cries of the wolf, of rivers in Minnesota, of views and life on the Mississippi, of a small stream in Southeast Minnesota called the Root, of the beauty up in northern Idaho. I was reminded of my home state, Iowa, where I grew up, of calm surroundings. I was reminded of the real things I needed to get started with as a New Native. I understood, even further, other writers such as Wendell Berry, Denise Low, Gary Snyder, Barry Lopez, Wes Jackson, all of whom speak repeatedly, and reverently about rediscovering a homeland; and of creating a style of self sufficiency and sense of place. To quote from Wes Jackson's book, *Becoming Native To This Place* (Kentucky, 1994), *"Our task is to build cultural fortresses to protect our emerging nativeness...to assume the awesome responsibility to both validate and educate those who want to be homecomers — not necessarily to go home but to go someplace and dig in and begin the long search and experiment to become native."*

---

[17] The comparison of a river to an elixir is quite interesting. The Alchemists (of whom I feel connected to in the way I view and interact with the world most of the time) felt an elixir could extend life forever (which literally is a painful concept, but as a sense of hope quite intriguing). They also thought of an elixir as part of the ingredient that could turn other materials into gold. A river, as a thing, thought of as capable of transformation into a more desired attitude or item is quite useful. Perhaps trout are the result of a life in the elixir of water. If I ever have the chance to name a flow of water I believe I will call it the Elixir River, or Elixir Creek. [Note also, in regards to alchemy, Denise Low's book *Tulip Elegies: An Alchemy of Writing* (Penthe)].

As I sat watching images tumble through my head by the Rogue River, I felt strange and uneasy. I was being told something. I could make out a word, being whispered, and it was "almost." I was almost right about Oregon, but river water is, for me, only halfway. A partner to the Sycamore tree, the Oak tree, the Sugar Maple, the Walnut tree, stunted hillsides, flat cornfields. Hardwood and crickets were calling for me in the water of the Rogue. No person can tell me what a river can tell me. A river has only honesty and truth to express. Use the river nearest you as a soothsayer and be tempted into, out of, or along your journey.

Concentrating on a river eases stress and straightens thought. A river can mend the nostalgia for faraway friends and family, open new hopes, and settle hypothetical intuitions. A river will often be so consoling that it will literally enter a person: bring tears to eyes. Rivers are like that. If you haven't sat alone, in the early morning, along a river and thought, you must do so soon. You will be surprised at what you find in your mind. Perhaps a most impossible, long lost thought will surface.

Don't get carried away though. A river is not a crystal ball. The most you can hope for is to admire, possibly get a few tips. Yet, trust whatever may come your way.

Writing about rivers is painfully constricting. I would love to take readers by the hand and lead them to a river, where they could watch, jump in, splash, or at least hear the rumbling-tumbling noises, but all I have are words to try and lead the way. Rivers are simply truth. They are almost understandable for this reason.

WALK ON WATER

Right now I am remembering an event I had yesterday, when I watched trout rising and falling within water which seemed invisible.

I look at river water sometimes and can't find it (I see the ground but nothing in between, or see what I think is the ground and nothing below). I had this experience when seeing Crater Lake for the first time. I couldn't find it. I wonder, how is this possible? How can a whole lake, that provides life to fish, insects, and complex varieties of surrounding plant life disappear.

I am reminded, in complete and utter humility, of the episode, so well known in western religion, of being able to walk on water. It is hard to discern if this skill is truly fact or fiction. I am close to understanding this act from time to time. To walk on water is as confounding as finding water gone. Perhaps, the secret rests in either an abundance of, or lack of faith. Limitations of thought can limit possibilities, but the disappearance of all the water in Crater Lake could have very easily sent me walking over what others knew as a deep and beautiful body of water.

DON'T EVEN THINK ABOUT IT

Where the water of rivers start, continue, and end, in all directions: headwaters, endwaters, delta, mouth, upstream, downstream, rain, snow, draw, gulch, humidity. How water enters the mind; how it works into memory; why it flows along the path it does; where fish come from—all of these are questions I never bother to try and answer, but I must admit I ask them all the time.

If you must have answers about rivers I pity you. Take my word for it. If you must have answers you had best try something else than rivers, like monitoring sunrises and sunsets, or investing money in a fixed interest savings account for thirty to forty years. A river changes and stays the same at each moment. This is the extent of what I believe.

A POOR PLACE TO TRY AND FORD
I'll try and blatantly define a river once. Only once though, because I refuse to be humiliated, so shamelessly abused, to show how hard it is. A river is as fleeting as the current it maintains.

The river seems to start much further away than my eyes and ears. The beginning of a river is the root of where my feelings of worship come from. Perhaps the river corresponds to humans in this way: the spot where the river begins may also be the spot where the ability for human worship initiates. Where is that, you ask? My best answer, sometimes. Sometimes from above tree line. Sometimes in the slow accumulation of rain. Sometimes out of a gushing spring. (Underground? Think about that. In a search for answers it's not even fair for the river to play without visible, well-lighted rules, but thankfully it does.)

Do this: take away the sometimes—above tree line, in the slow accumulation of rain, out of a gushing spring...it doesn't matter, descriptions are useless. (Or try adding almost.) Even if I felt I'd found the beginning of a river. Walked up where snow was seemingly melting and starting a creek. I would still be faced with more, for I also realize that the river is not merely the water, or the flow, or the banks that it follows. The river goes much beyond, and deeper than these categories at every instant that it exists. (Surely it's not this hard to understand, one thinks. But a canal has flow, banks, water, but it is most definitely NOT a river.) Consider this, even a reflection of a river has many of the obvious characteristics of a river (and actually more characteristics than a canal).

I like to think of a river as a work of art in many ways and as in art, the answers, or the "truth," as such, is never known because it is arrived at through interpretation. Since interpretation is a constantly changing concept, meanings, like that of the river (or of art, or literature), is never understood completely and, although frustrating, it is, for its changing qualities, best that way.[18]

A river extends interpretation because it will let someone monitor it with numbers if they want. A person can study the river scientifically for years and when done, have a document with many references in hand declaring knowledge. Yet, with document in hand, this person could stroll innocently to the shore of a stream and discover something completely new, way beyond any numeric value they may have previously settled on or interpolated. After all, there are rivers within rivers really.

---

[18] I must give full credit for what little understanding I have of aesthetics, theories of art, and interpretation to Allan Megill in his book *Prophets of Extremity* (California, 1986).

The surface current of a river is moving much faster than the current of water at the bottom of a river. The break up of rocks in a river is constant yet always varied. The river can be summed up quite well with a phrase from eastern thought, out of Lao Tzu's *The Way of Life*, "The way is easy, strive hard."

THE DOSEWALLIPS RIVER
One never expects it to be so hard.

Spontaneity is partly true as it fleets by.

There is no way that I expected the river to be so difficult to know in the beginning. My first revelation of this came in the Olympic National Park, along the West Fork of the Dosewallips River. (The perfect name in my opinion.) The word dosewallips hints at a mean punch, a cross between Muhammad Ali and Mike Tyson, with necessary medical attention needed soon after. I can imagine a cartoon, during a fight scene, where instead of writing WHAM, or BASH, they would write DOSEWALLIPS!!

At the time of my downfall, I was brilliant enough to believe I could figure out everything in the world. Thought that I could explain all things with deep, mind-altering-poetic prose. I sat down by a bank of the Dosewallips and got thrashed in my attempt to figure out the flow of water; rivers. All I remember is writing about what the river wasn't and feeling humiliated, that the best I could do was decipher something barely even vague, yet I still believed, even more so, in the river after my embarrassment. I have never forgotten that experience. I cherish the West Fork of the Dosewallips for this marvelous lesson of impossibility.

EVENT 2 — WILLIAM STAFFORD READS "ASK ME"
"What the river says, that is what I say." — William Stafford

A second event, soon after the Dosewallips. I heard William Stafford read, in person, his poem, "Ask Me," which confirmed that it is good to trust what one can't understand. I marveled at the preamble he gave this poem. He told us how he was approached in a restaurant, a coastal one I believe, by a waitress who asked if he was William Stafford. He said he was. Shortly after, the waitress returned, with her husband (a cook in the back) and they both said to him, "Are you the one who wrote, 'Ask Me'? We both love that poem." What a great way to be known.

Anyway, he told us that he would read the poem as slowly as he could, but that he could never read it slowly enough in his opinion. This poem definitely helped me understand and gain trust in the realm of rivers. His poem speaks reverently and trustingly in the mystery of water. Confirming truth in mystery.

These two incidents, so close together, combined with many other things previous and since, have bolstered my faith in rivers. I have been following them, studying them and thinking of them my whole life, but the Dosewallips and William Stafford made them stand out with distinction, set my obsessions even more a blaze. Now I have become attached, hopelessly, to the banks of rivers as sources of refuge, mystery and glory.

The rivers close to me as I work on this now (I enjoy saying their names, so will, the Wood, the Sprague, Spring Creek, the Williamson, The Klamath, the Sycan, the Rogue, and now in Iowa, Spring Branch Creek and the Root, to name the close ones) are so clear, cold, and beautiful that I can hardly believe my eyes and ears: they are literally grace. By grace I mean the smooth process and presentation of a thing, in conjunction with surroundings. Grace is an expression much beyond words, reliant upon a trust in the invisible, needing faith. May you be blessed by Saint River and feel its grace. Sight, feeling, thought and touch merged in to one.

The Wood River

The first time I saw the Wood River, up at its very cold headwaters in southern Oregon, where it springs forth from the ground, I tipped my hat and drew in a long breath. I said to my wife, "Amazing! Absolutely amazing. Holy Krips!"[19] We both looked, helplessly, at the entire situation.

Because we're human we had to start somewhere with the thing. We couldn't let it be, ignore it, pretend it didn't exist. We had to involve ourselves physically with the river. We by no means attacked it. We walked along it for a long while, around many long curves and viewed the entire region that we could see from where we stood, way down low and from far away. I got out my water filter (I am not sure I needed it, but am cautious all the

---

[19] "Holy Krips," is a strange phrase I use, an alteration of Holy Shit perhaps, but much more powerful. Plus, as the title of the book would hint, the Wood River is everything I could hope for in a name.

same) and drew each of us a cold, very cold, drink. We had a lunch along the banks, stared and marveled longer and decided that I would fish, and she would hike the banks.

I am not, by any means, proficient at fly fishing. I lack common sense for one thing. My natural ability to use my mind as an asset disappears the closer I get to the flow of water. I loose basic psychomotor skills: I can barely tie knots and I trip as I walk. My vocabulary shrinks to about five words: Wow, Dang, Man, Ugh, and Hmm. Characteristics like these are some of the best things about a good river. I lose myself entirely. Usually after two or three hours I recover some of my senses, and I hate that. It is wicked to recover from illusion and joy.

I would say I go against the preconceived notion of the patient, calm, ultra-pasturized fly fisherman image. Rivers and fly casting excite me far too much to project myself as a calm, pipe-smoking, tweed-wearing, tenured English professor. I cast and flick and mutter (with my small, five-word river vocabulary) in a sort of static-filled manner, making whooshing and air-blown sound effects the entire time. If it weren't for the fact that I catch fish from time to time I would assume that I scare them all away. Sometimes I think my perception of the water, my approval and attempts to move like water birds help me more than any fly pattern I try to fish with. After all, the flies I tie aren't really very accurate imitations and are based primarily on the trout's inherent behavior of excitability. I always fish with the idea in mind that if I place an interesting enough item, sometimes out of character, of the right color, in front of the right fish, something will happen. In carpenter's terms, I like to think that I am enough off plumb that I can get away with these bad habits.

I have been to both the headwaters and the tailwaters of the Wood River and many points in between. It flows well, it seems to sprout grasshoppers, and it has good fish in it. The views out from it, while on a canoe for instance, are magnificent. I feel inadequate even describing it. I would need to be like Shakespeare to explain water and rivers like the Wood. I want to describe it with running flows of rhythmic rhyme, free and current-driven, forward into time. Merging distance and thought as one, in circles, made of movement. For me, at good times, all the world's a river, carried well within the flow of water: *"Like as waves make towards the pebbled shore, So do our minutes hasten to their end; Each changing place with that which goes before, In sequent toil all forwards do contend"* (Shakespeare's Sonnets 60, l. 1-4).

THE WESTERN CULT OF UNDERSTATEMENT: A RIVER ISN'T A CREEK, OR VICE VERSA

In Missoula, Montana, I had my first encounter with water understatement. I was attending a writing conference in the hub of liberal, free-wheeling Montana, when I went fishing (which I must admit far outshined the writing conference), along the banks of Rock Creek. When I first saw the flow of water I kind of laughed to myself. My writing (fishing?!) partner and I both thought and said the same thing I am sure, "A creek in Montana is bigger than a river in Kansas." I don't know how many cubic feet of water were flowing, madly, in Rock Creek, but I was impressed for many reasons: the motion of the water, the excitement of good (but hard) fishing and an awesome surrounding landscape.

We caught a fair number of fish and still wondered, stepping over slapping beaver tails, watching herons, kingfishers, and imitating the noise of rumpus raven, how this creek could be so labeled. It roared like a mighty river.

A Creek Defined

When I was a little child in Iowa my image of a creek came into existence, and I shall hold on to it, even though Montana, Idaho, and Oregon have tried to take it away from me, calling rivers creeks.

In Iowa City I lived in a part of town that allowed me and my friends to play in the woods. They really were, too; at least until the Dutch Elm Disease took a bite. Then some of the woods became vacant, but still, there were many trees. We were isolated from town on all sides and regularly saw wildlife: deer, opossum, owls, raccoons, groundhogs, turkey; found mushrooms; made forts with sticks and bark; and most of all played in the creek.

The creek was a small trickle of water. Tiny. One step across, yet somehow it flowed all year into the much larger, and appropriately named, Iowa River. We used to make dams that expanded the creek into a pond, which we called so. We made ponds so big that we couldn't even run and jump over them. To put ponds into perspective, we didn't ice skate on ponds, when we went ice skating we went to lakes.

Anyway, summer, fall and spring (sometimes winter) we were involved with the creek. We created flows of water that ran over rocks. The creek would look so good trickling over the rocks, we would drink the water and declare it the best water we had ever tasted. My best friend said that he and his family drank creek water in Colorado like this and never got sick, so we gulped down more and more. I am not sure why, but we never got sick on the creek water in Iowa, although, later, we had a feeling that most of the water flowing down the creek was run-off from the streets and included some septic drainings. Interestingly enough, we never confirmed this, or even tried to discover the very beginnings of this creek. I don't think we wanted to know. We cherished our lives along the creek far too much to want to understand it in any way other than good. When it rained nothing could have even begun to keep us from racing down to watch the water rise.

I suppose a kid who grows up in Western Montana would consider my idea of a creek a draw, or a gully. Not a serious flow of water where they could ever learn to play and have fun. For an Iowa kid (Iowegian) though, a creek will always be a tiny little sprig of water that lets you play and get wet in all year round.

WHAT RIVERS SOUND LIKE, PART ONE
How do you whisper so soft and clear that you're heard across a noisy room anyway? Is it possible that an F-16 jet plane, cruising far ahead of its sound, is a close

approximation of the sound a water fall makes as it drops smooth strands of mist and air, slowly, through a narrow crevice in the Cascade Mountains?

River noise is wispy, quirky. When you round a single corner, on a path, near a river, the noise of the water can sound as loud as a rocket exploding. Walk three more steps, around a small bend, and you may not even know a river exists.

It seems to me that the noise of a river travels in fewer directions than other sounds. Most noises expel outwards, up, down, and sideways, yet, like the mist on a cold morning in the summer, the noise of a river only travels up, beyond the tips of Redwood trees. If this is true, then perhaps this explains the noise of thunder, which is the accumulated sound of rivers stored up in the sky, forced straight back, down to the earth's surface, with the help of lightning.

The Sound of Rivers, Part Two

Juxtaposition. Take a dog barking (ugh), a baby crying (almost ugh), a souped-up, 4-wheel-drive pickup, including gun racks, never taken out of city limits (super ugh), and tell me you wouldn't hear these noises through a stand of trees, over on the other side of a hill. The noise that water makes is like the comparison between a push mower and a gas mower, a chain saw and a hand saw, a wooden paddle and a gas motor. One fits in, the other doesn't.[20] I am once again taken to the idea of

---

[20] This idea of an appropriate noise within context is not new. It was passed along to me from an essay by Wendell Berry in *Home Economics*, titled "Getting Along With Nature" (North Point Press, 1987).

grace and assimilation. Rivers want to hide and do so partly by camouflaging the noise they make, imitating the sound of falling leaves, of squirrels digging in leaves, or of birds flying. Nothing presents itself so humbly as a river. A river is easy on the ear.

LET WATER RUN WIDE AND SLOW THROUGHOUT THE DRY

"I will pour water upon him that is thirsty, and floods upon dry ground: I will pour my spirit upon thy seed, and my blessing upon thine offspring: and they shall spring up as among the grass, as willows by the water courses" (Isiah, 45, 3-4).

The one aspect that I think of, when I think of the author Wallace Stegner, is his reference to the Western Regions of the United States and their characteristic absence of water.[21] When one thinks of the way the West deals with water, this becomes obvious. Water is both cherished and abused; at some point I hope for it to be respected. You hear about water being sold to Los Angeles for the next twenty years. Of water in Montana being piped off to big cities. In a slack year, I suppose, some of the sold-off rivers technically run dry, the water being accounted for before it even starts to flow, melt, or fall from the sky.

---

[21] There is definitely a fear of open space and lack of water that wants to captivate the human mind. My first observation of this was driving across western Iowa to Nebraska with a couple of friends. One of my friends was from Wyoming and the other from Vermont. The one from Wyoming was feeling more and more at ease as we drove into more wide open country. The friend from Vermont was slowly getting, more and more concerned as the sky and land opened up, threatening to take over.

When you mention buying land in the West, one of the first comments someone pops at you is, "Does it have a well?" As one wanders the dry regions of the West, Midwest, or any region characteristically void of water, the wish for wet nourishment runs rampant, and hints of psychotic obsession surface—the eyes start to see what they want. Basic necessities are not forgotten in a dry land, which is good.

If it's a drought, crazy ideas take over about when and how it will rain. Why rain isn't arriving will be discussed. The most common things said these days are: "The greenhouse effect has sure changed our place. Why, I remember ten years ago it always used to rain...." There is also the stand-by (and real) theory regarding the Ozone Layer, and about every third year, if there are droughts or floods, people mention the El Nino factor. People use these theories as they do when explaining the winning or losing streaks of baseball teams, as if there is nothing they can do (although speaking as if they do know what to do), implying it's the way things are. Which is not really correct in some ways, but may be in others. After all, if the ozone is the problem, it could have been completely avoided and could still be slowly reversed in some ways, using the Fixer Mentality.

People always tend to glorify the past, dotting their memories with the few extremes that stand out. Yet the talk of "a stretch of bad weather," does seem more relevant these days as regions which used to get thick blankets of snow, like eastern Kansas, don't anymore. The oral history of weather can explain the well-being of a town about as well as the oral history of the local high school football team. It would be interesting if towns posted on their greeting signs, alongside State Athletic Championships, a statement about their weather.

A lot of the time, in the Midwest especially, since unlike out West where a lack of water is much more real, kids and parents often joke about rain dance rituals and the *Farmer's Almanac* during strange weather. People take water and rivers for granted and treat them with less obvious respect on a personal and daily basis in the East and northern Midwest areas. The West mixes more pride in with their rivers, but also turns around and exploits them with far more abandon it seems to me. It is safe to say that the West by no means has a strangle hold on water abuse, just a better knack for reckless abandon. Although, a trip to the Ohio river basin or the lower Mississippi would scare the living day lights out of the concept clean water.

Watch someone water their lawn (the most ridiculous thing I know of, since not only is it a waste of water, but then you have to spend time mowing the grass, which is also a waste of time and a waste of energy), and you are watching a strange ritual of cultured waste. In Washington State, east of the Cascades, the State Parks seem obsessed with having green grass everywhere. You can't even pitch your tent on the grass in some campgrounds, you must sleep on gravel they prize the grass so much. What's so wrong with sage and brown grass? How can you appreciate an area if you don't respect what it offers? Of course, I am not surprised by this behavior. After all, most of what people think of as love and marriage follow these lines. People love what they see, not what really exists: blind love leads, in turn, to bad marriages between people and the environment.

Consider the promise of a river running through a dryer region of the West. Where this occurs, you have a truly blessed region. To wish for blessing is to wish for life. The Columbia River Gorge sparkles, east, beyond the Cascades with river water. The Deschutes River flows with brilliance through the High Desert region of Oregon. It is easy to understand how more earthly religions would feel blessed in proximity to such water. The idea of an Oasis is possible. A mirage comes true. Rivers are one of the few items that can produce miracles. It doesn't rid a desert region of its obvious dryness to have water course through, but it does offer hope and the prospects of a sort of unreal, illusionary, diversity.

SALT LAKE CITY: THE CONCEPT AND THE PLACEMENT

For some, when you think of salt and water you begin to spit. For those in Salt Lake City, they begin to live. I have a fear of and a soft spot for Salt Lake City. Good people tell me it is good. I must believe them. Yet I quiver with the thought of the place. Salt water in the dry desert. I can't help it—the place holds no charm for me. My car always has problems when I approach the place. I sweat all over with anxiety. When I start the eastward ascent up and away, into Wyoming, my car and my body start to feel better again. I applaud those who can live there. I can't, however, fully imagine why a clump of people would live there. It is water. It is life. It is a Holy Place, a place of water and I grant these things. I promise, as well, to leave it alone.

47

Damn Dams

Edward Abbey would shudder in his grave to hear of any support for dams. For instance, to dam up and flood any more of the Klamath River watershed would be a shame.

Honestly look at both sides and try to conceive which argument makes sense: to dam or not to dam. I am obviously blind. I don't support dams. However, there are good arguments for the building of dams. You can't disagree with them all. Dams provide power. They provide a large number of people with recreation. It can be argued that lakes are aesthetically beautiful. I am one of those who can't visualize the beauty of a dammed river. When I see a dam I see what is below the water first and think of the tricks being played on water temperature. Dammed-up rivers make me see a beautiful valley, silted over and gone forever. I think of salmon unable to swim. I have no empathy for the gods of electricity and recreation in relation to the abuse of rivers. One could easily use sun power and learn to ride in boats not powered by loud, ugly, gas motors. I concede there is more to it than this, but I prefer not to know. My mind is made up for better or for worse. Facts, or no facts.

The Big Rivers

Mention big rivers and I immediately think Mississippi, Columbia, Penobscot. I know there are probably others, but these, so far, are the Big Rivers to me. I dare any man, woman, or child, heck, even animal, not to at least sneak a peek at the Mississippi River when you cross it over one of the many bridges, south of Dubuque, Iowa.

Even the most blasé of non-nature-loving, gung-ho, financial, *Star Trek* freaks will lift their heads for a glance, whereupon a small clicking of a micron of a synapses, deep in the brain, will bleep a tone of acknowledgment, whether repressed or overt, into a yelp, when off the tongue will emit, "Wow! Big River."

You come around a corner in the state of Washington, down a hill, going west, say towards Portland, Oregon from Pullman, Washington, on past the tri-cities of Washington, and along the way you will see a big swath of water. If it's evening and the sun's going down, you'll see a bronzed view of the Columbia, the majestic flow of the Northwest. Once, on a trip to Maine, I crossed the Penobscot and felt similar awe at the size of this river as I crossed.

What is the difference between one of the big rivers and other rivers? For one thing, a new word ought to be declared. Something more appropriate like Bargewake, Bountiver, or Catastrophiver.

Along the Mississippi, up near the tip of Northeast Iowa, where Minnesota and Wisconsin all join, there are sub-rivers within the river, bridges across the river that go from island to island. The Big Rivers offer a much more complex environment. When, for instance, I look at the Columbia River and contemplate how I would fly fish it, I get emotionally disturbed. When I try to grasp the Mississippi, I get annoyed at how inconceivable it is to understand. Even with the Missouri River (not what I would call one of the big ones, but surely a rare river in its length and width, from its headwaters up in Montana, to its polluted garble, many miles later in Missouri) I get

49

confused. About the biggest river I can handle is the Klamath River, and do so with a struggle twenty to thirty miles downstream from Klamath Falls, Oregon.

CONVERSATION STYLES FOR MEN TO USE ALONG RIVERS

When you stand next to a river you don't approach full of conversation, you might say, "Nice river," or "Now that's a river."

Try to be calm when speaking about a river, especially around older men. You can begin to get excited, only, if say, the people you are talking to are college kids and there are many of them and what you say probably won't be heard anyway.

Another tip. When you walk up on men along a good river, it's even better if you don't mention the river at all. It's too obvious. Say, instead, "Good day, huh?" Or perhaps, "Not a bad trail they got going down here?"

If you're a guy, and you meet a lady along a river DO NOT agree that the river is cute. No matter what. It is only slightly acceptable to agree that the river is pretty. If you are younger, or if the female is younger (preferably under six years old, but flirting is allowed, even though you will regret it later), you are allowed to disrespect the river, briefly, but not honestly, and utter, "Yep, I guess." in response to the comment of cute, but still, never actually say the word cute, or all the River Gods of the Universe and all the men of the world will brutally beat you to a pulp. You will be marked for life, so don't dare utter the word.

If you're a dad, an adult male and/or potential male role-model, make an effort to avoid lecturing kids on what the river is factually, or has been historically. Kids have far less respect for facts than a few, interesting interpretations dressed up with a touch of truth.[22]

FOLKS THAT TAKE ADVANTAGE OF PUBLIC LAND
ALONG RIVERS

This is strictly my own political view, but people who shack-up along rivers, on public land areas such as National Forests, BLM land, National Parks, and what-not are misbehaving. It is hard to wish for them a true, homesteading, back-to-nature experience. It takes much effort and commitment to keep rivers wild and scenic. For a very few to camp out on them for months, to build fires (a very serious and inevitable forest fire threat), no doubt poaching, and using the water to wash in, clean dishes in, to urinate and defecate near, or in, is not independence, but selfish and destructive. I suggest you always bring such people to the attention of the authorities. This will make the authorities at least check on areas they probably never go to and may keep the rivers a bit cleaner.[23]

Too many people in the world, unfortunately, requires more monitoring. To see a few ding-bats exploit pristine areas (especially pristine rivers which we have very little of) is chagrining. It makes me upset even to write about it now. Don't stand for these posed acts of individualism that reek of selfish exploitation.

---

[22] A valuable idea I garnered from Barry Lopez's essay "Children in the Woods," from *Crossing Open Ground* (Vintage, 1989).

[23] I would recommend confronting these people alone, but this could pose serious hazards to your health at times.

"Verily, verily, I say unto thee; Except a man be born of water and of the Spirit, he cannot enter into the Kingdom of God" (John 3:5).

It is no mistake that water is held sacred and that it is thought of as a source of birth and resurrection. Sometimes I prefer to think of the power of water as that of the Spirit of Shapeshifting. The ability to shift, metamorphosize, between solids, gases, and liquids. A river is somewhat of a fleeting glimpse at all times.

Symbolically one may understand the strangle that water has over people by viewing polluted, dirty, hot water, like the Ganges, and learning that this water is considered very Holy. Sacred. It would be like finding out that rusty, smelly, organic waste in a city land fill was the center of worship for people living in cushy suburbs. Not wrong, but unexpected. Devotion is where it comes from, supported internally within the mind, and is captivating. Symbolic belief is blind, but reassuring to those involved. Hyperbolic acts of devotion to something so seemingly non-sacred to our clean and polished, cultivated minds is frustrating.

What makes sense to us? John the Baptist. Shoving people's heads into the water, backwards. Saving and bringing one to the possibility of a holy life.

In Buddhist literature, Siddhartha crosses the river and is realized on the other side.

I often imagine that Rip Van Winkle's awakening is related to a river. Perhaps, in his long dream state he dreamed of crossing water and that signaled his time to wake up again.

One explanation could be that most of the Holy Water stories are latent hopes, manifested out of desert heat. Do people in the rain forest think water is Holy? Of course, but probably in a different way. Abundance makes the mind think differently. Polytheism is valuable in this way. Where does the Sun God rank in relation to the Rain God in comparison to a local bio-region?

Do natives to the Mississippi, or the Columbia River, feel the same about water? I wonder if they would consider washing in dirty, hot liquid like those along the Ganges. These are not questions of right and wrong; they are questions about the values placed upon water in a Holy sense. Different cultures praise and admire water differently, but all cultures admire rivers and water. So when Norman Maclean titled his book, *A River Runs Through It*, he was right on.

WATER STUDY TECHNIQUES

I have a feeling that water flows universally and that watching about any water with a current, which from time to time creates bubbling, splashing, or dripping, can help you better understand larger rivers.

My theory is that of the Bonsai Tree. Studying small creeks can lead you to better figure out flow and motion. Pooling actions.

I suppose it's not much different than placing a micro in the realm of a macro. I was hiking in a wilderness area, along a very small creek in Western Oregon, when I stood still and felt this whole concept emerge. The tiny creek had slowly dug down, in proportion to the height of its cliffs, nearly twenty times its width. From time to time I spotted a bit of soil, a grain of dirt, fall into the flow. The light bits of nearby pollen would blow and drift into the water. The whole process is much like flying. You get an overview, such as what a bird gets flying over the Big Two Hearted River. Such perspectives can help in understanding.

Wind and Tulip Bulbs: The Sound of Rivers, Part Three

Laugh if you want, but I am convinced of one thing. The wind is planted, harvested and comes to life in rivers. It is seeded in the evening and sprouts in the morning, usually starting in the east, where, strangely enough, wind is born. Much of the pebble matter you spot along rivers then, are bulbs, like tulips, that open up and hatch air, forced through the water, in bursts. There is no question about this. It is something I am sure of. Ask me why and I'll have no specific explanation. I may, if pushed, mention a rare form of egg algae found in some spring creeks as proof, but my lack of material evidence doesn't make my claim false. Surprise is knowledge's victory.

Beware of Your River Friends

I suggest you keep your river friends confined to rivers, streams, and creeks. You'll be surprised how Coyote wraps your visions and makes the people you like fishing with, canoeing with, sailing with, the most ugly cretins in the universe when back on land, in a house, in the city, or anywhere away from the water. Water brings repressed, self-centered, super-hero qualities to a person. They say things they would never say otherwise, or utter comments they will later regret, trying to be cool, while caught up in fake bonding. If you recognize this in yourself or in others there's no need to flee, or be scared. Understand that the river has a strange hold on people. It promotes grandeur. You will probably have a great time with your river friends, but like vinegar and oil, you will feel a bit uneasy with what they have said, will say, or might do off the water. Agree to meet them only on river banks.

I would even avoid driving to a river together. However, I've found that driving together, to and fro, can be a good time of transition.

A River Made from Scratch

Close your eyes. Imagine the "perfect" river. It will be one you've seen before. Perhaps not the one you expect it to be.

When I was about fifteen I didn't really know what the mountains were like. I had this desire to see a mountain stream. My parents asked my brother and me where we wanted to go for vacation and I took control, "Colorado, the Rocky Mountains." Thank God that's where we went. We went to Rocky Mountain National Park and did many things. We met some of my parents' friends, who liked the mountains also. I had become interested in photography and this interest, teamed, with my desire to backpack and see water sent me around the place like a super ball. We walked down a trail, from tundra, to our camp area and followed a stream. I believe I took somewhere between 75-100 pictures in about an hour and a half. I was snapping and focusing faster than a motor drive would have been able to wind the film.

My dad's friend, who was along for the walk, is an avid photographer as well. He showed me tips on how to frame a picture, how to slow the shutter to get the flow of water. I raced off and took another roll of film. I think I was obsessed because I didn't want to let go of the water. I had envisioned water, trickling and flowing for so long from Iowa that I wanted to keep the mountain stream with me forever.

Where this admiration of mountain water came from I have never been able to explain. I guess I was born with a desire to watch and be with flowing water. This trip to Colorado is the first time I remember feeling an obsession for rivers. It sparked out of me from nowhere, and has never died out.

In regards to my pictures. They weren't really all that great in the end, but a few were. Of course, that wasn't the point. The point, I believe, now, was not that I wanted to take the river with me—it was wanting to be involved with the water intensely. I wasn't satisfied with only looking. I wanted to be examining it, looking at bits of it, listening. Although, I am sure I wouldn't have complained if, when I got back to Iowa, the Big Thompson River had decided to follow me home.

The Without-Water River

Some people call it the Badlands. The part of South Dakota that I am fascinated with. It is, to me, the River Without Water. The hallucinogenic, bold and curvy landscape reflects moonlight day and night. It tremors in the early spring, and stuns you with the feeling that rivers do. It's not that you can't find water there, you just forget about it. It feels like it may be all around you, that if you pushed on the edges of what you can see—the crusty soil and open grass plains—that a gush of liquid would flow all around you.

Once, the sun shining and the temperature rising to the high nineties, I laid down in a small stream in the Badlands, and when I got out I was white like chalk dust. I think of this Badland's creek as the driest creek I've ever been to, a slough of wet dust.

In the Badlands, Bison roam relatively free, as do coyotes and hawks. I've heard talk of the mountain sheep, have never seen them, but most definitely believe they exist. The region feels like being in a bubble floating down a river the way it rolls and yells of freedom.

The Badlands mesmerize you with landscape and water synchronicity. A landscape painter, and friend of mine, can paint the Badlands so well that it's frightening. He makes you wonder if he isn't part Badlands. But what I am reminded of, when I see his paintings of the Badlands (besides good times), is what I imagine a small portion of a river would look like if you could stretch it apart: if you could tug at the edges of a pool of water and stretch it over a canvas. The curves, the surface tension battles going on at each moment on a river alongside sunlight and reflections of clouds, are similar to the way the Badlands look up close and from a distance.

The River Disappears

In the National Sand Dunes park of southern Colorado, the river disappears in to the sand. Is it the clouds that suck the water up so fast in the dry climate? Perhaps the water is frightened to be so exposed, in an area where it makes no sense to be. However, it is magnificent to see water, granted no more than a trickle, running along the top of sand. The small trickle of water approximates the fine, innermost progression of an Ocean wave crashing up into the land. Maybe there is a tunnel from the Pacific Ocean to the Sand Dunes in Colorado and what happens is the water drains through the earth, from say, the mid coast of California, and then back into the ocean again from the Sand Dunes. The next time I visit the Sand Dunes I'll have to taste the water, I have a small inkling that it will taste salty.

Rivers and Lakes in Northern Minnesota

Wolf lets you know where you are, but not where he is. The water is brilliant in Northern Minnesota. There are loons that flabbergast you. They say you will rarely, if ever, see a wolf in the wild. But don't think that this means you haven't been seen by one. I have only seen wolf prints. Monster dog marks is how I reconcile what I call wolf prints. Yet when canoeing and hearing a wolf cry out, I feel like I can see their reflections in the water. I am fairly certain that, once, I saw the lingering reflection of a wolf in the water, where it had recently finished drinking.

What would this mean? What if water were an absorber of an area. If it could hold what it reflected, to be seen later. Would this still be the same as seeing an animal in the wild? Of course, maybe you think this is possible, that you can see a wolf in the water. Maybe, after two weeks of hearing a wolf, you'll become convinced that the wolf is such a master of disguising itself, that it hides as the reflection of a tree. I can think of no reason why a wolf isn't capable of this.

I am reminded of this wildness in Northern Minnesota by simply catching blue gills on a fly rod. Blue gills bite like a carnival of surprise in these northern lakes. It is conceivable that these normally small fish are strengthened by the howls of wolf. It seems possible that these fish are concentrated globs of wolf reflection and howls.

Mention Minnesota and I will always think like this. Of wolves and water, teamed together, forming a mystery I can never get enough of. Getting in this water is to be by the wolf, and it makes me wild. A region of unconsciousness: water and wolf, bordered well with trees.

SWIMMING TO MEXICO: WETBACKS

The idea is baffling. When I was little my grandparents lived down along the U.S.- Mexico Border, in Eagle Pass, Texas. Once, staying at a relative's house, we went north of Del Rio, to a river cabin, and what was amazing was where the river took us. I jumped in with my brother and we swam to Mexico. We stood on the opposite shore and waved to my grandfather who was on the back porch, watching, kind of laughing at us I think. Would we want to stay?

It is a strange concept, a river that divides so much, and the two of us on the other side. I laugh when I think of us two little kids, big grins, doing something we knew was wrong and crazy, but so easy and fun.

In this same region, on my grandfather's ranch, I found out the difference between irrigation ditches and rivers. I didn't know the difference then. His catfish pond was filled and stocked through irrigation, as was the water he used for washing and watering. He did this by pumping the water from his catfish pond into a couple large holding tanks. The drinking water was obtained from the hospital where my grandfather was the Mechanical Engineer. When we visited, we filled up fifty to sixty plastic gallon jugs. I would say that my grandfather paid respect to the ways of water quite a bit. He had a very complex and utilitarian relationship with water that still intrigues me to this day: the way he fashioned his lifestyle alongside pumps and irrigation.

CIGAR PARTY

Years ago. Went to Iowa, met with my friends. Did a drive up to Northeastern Iowa to do some trout fishing. We pulled out of town early to get there. Bought far too many dozens of bad donuts (a poor idea as part of our ritual) and coffee for the drive. The day before we had bought big, nasty cigars (an even worse part of the ritual we had developed). We would eat fish for dinner. We drove up to Bailey's Ford and fished for trout. We caught some, but our main topic of conversation was commenting on the bait of choice being used by those around us. Corn. A tip of Marshmallow, dried out with a bit of Salmon egg. I have no idea what we were using to catch fish. I found others' bait amusing. I sure hope we weren't using marshmallows though. That would tarnish my current fly fishing pride.

In Iowa, on the tinier spring fed streams, people pay almost no attention to the water. Which is a shame, because some of the streams are fair representatives of good, clean water. People more or less figure out the fish stocking schedule and then drive around, about an hour behind, simply regathering the trout. If, however, it's been a few hours since the stock truck came by and you catch a fish, you might as well move out because, from amidst shadows, folks (we called them the people from Cedar Rapids) will take over your spot. When you catch a fish, you might as well shout, "YO Everybody, Over Here, Fish." If you really want to watch people squirm in Iowa, you can do one thing that makes mouths drop open. You see, it really pains people in Iowa to see you toss a fish back in the water. "What you fishing for?" they'll ask.[24]

On this particular trip I didn't want to clean the fish, or for that matter keep any of them. Heck, I was irritated when fish got on the end of my line. I wanted to be alone. When I did catch a fish, I was letting them loose, but away from where I caught them, taking them over to the larger stream nearby where fewer people fished.

---

[24] One good thing about Iowa trout fishing is that the season is open all year. Thus, if you go in the bad times of year, you will see no one, you will be joined instead, by eagles, deer and snowflakes. They have also started catch and release areas, with artificial flies as well.

As for cleaning the fish we did keep, my friend did most of this. Next we cooked the trout with eggs and lemon, preparing one of those meals you never forget. We ate and kind of wished we had more. Then sat around a smoky fire, smoking our bad cigars. The only time anyone talked to us was when an old guy walked by and said, "Boy, I bet the mosquitoes aren't bothering you much, at least not in that stew pot you got going there." We knew he was referring to the smoky fire and the cigar smoke.

We could only have accomplished this type of trip on a river, behaving as river friends must from time to time.

HELD ABOVE MY HEAD FOREVER

I am talking about the North Platte River. You see it in Nebraska and Wyoming and I swear it goes over you. It sits high and sometimes wider than you would ever expect. I become sedate and calm when I get ready to enter the land of the North Platte River. It lifts my spirits instantly. It is a river that you could canoe up into the sky on. I am sure of it. I will have to check in the local history to see if this is rumored to have happened to anyone.

The North Platte River makes me think of Midwestern weather. The jet stream being the North Platte river in disguise, stewing together thunder, lightning and tornadoes; making the river flow above the ground once again, but with the potential of making rain and snow and wind.

Maybe it is all the cottonwood fluff that gets

absorbed into the water of the North Platte. All the liquid fluff makes the water lighter than air, allowing most of it to fly away somewhere across Nebraska. Sending invitations to the Sand Hill Cranes each year to keep them coming back.

WATER FALLS

The magnificent break in continuity roars and goes with abandon. Yet the waterfall is remarkably delicate if you watch its individual motions. Watch a single flop of water free-fall. It goes down in pure slow motion. Aerial assault it's not, except when all the water is viewed together as one.

Near the Columbia River is Multnomah Falls, on record, I believe, the second tallest fall in the United States. I must admit, even being right off the Interstate, outside Portland, Oregon, and preambled by a massive parking lot, the thing is still truly amazing. I am one of the people who has to walk down and be behind the base of the falling water in the off season. When you do so, you are most alone and impressed. The strength of a river to hold together, fall, pause a moment, then start flowing again, as if nothing had really happened, is confidence. Similar to a cat, which, when it falls, or makes a mistake, simply pauses then goes back to behavior as normal.

UNDERGROUND RIVERS

This concept makes me shake. What lurks in river water, down deep in caves, is probably stuff that glows in the dark.

There are the underground rivers of myth. These rivers mix the love of river water with the fear of what's deep under the ground. Claustrophobia sets in. Being buried in the earth is death. Mining in caverns isn't a habit one gets used to, or grows up with. It's not natural. It seems, I heard once, that most miners know someone that has died from being buried. Maybe it's my fearful self that thinks this bit of trivia to be true, but it seems very possible. I can imagine that many miners have lifelong coughs from dirt and cold air. Depth of earth and deep ocean water are strongly correlated to fear.

Yet put a river under the ground and you have the true potential for dialectic synthesis to occur. You get the comfort of river and the fear of underground. The results are neither comfort, nor fear.

Let's consider the river Styx. A spot where the dead were ferried by Charon to the land of Hades. The beauty of the river, perhaps suggested with the properties of dry ice exists. A tense mixture of life and death, hot and cold becomes imaginable. Opposites turned into one: the river and death.

Underground rivers are a source of extremes. Venture underground to the dead. A pleasant journey with a strange twist. Like I said, don't always trust your river friends away from water. They may want to take you underground, uncover their faces only to turn into Charon.

TRINITY RIVER
I only mention this river out of its glorious image in my mind. It flows through what is one of the most beautiful

regions of the country for me, the Trinity Alps in Northern California. I could never live here. It is overwhelming. I have caught good fish in this river, talked to many people I love and always will in this region. Found gold in the water, literally. I never forget this flow of water, even when I don't see it for years, or if I were never to see it again. It is my archetype for River. All rivers get unfairly compared with what I remember it to be.

Large Crystals of Exaggeration

He said to me, this lake is so big, that to dig it out we drove trucks with wheels as big as football fields. I was delirious, and I fully believed him, saying yes and nodding my head up and down without knowing any better. It was so hot that the coolant in my car was vapor. I had seen more water in front of me, on the road, than there was in the world. I knew they were mirages, but I sped up to try and find a splash anyway. Finally we stopped in a park along Lake Mead. That was when some guy, I assume he was real, came over, and told us about the big trucks and how this heat was nothing, he was going to put a sweater on because, you see, he explained, he was used to being in Death Valley. "Now," he said, "they got some real big trucks and equipment there and it's not so cold as here."

I felt him to be pounding and rambling. I wanted to yell out what I heard a crazy dude yell at slow moving cars near Nevada City, California, "Slow Down!" My arms twitching, my lips quaking. My jaw bone going between slack and vibrant.

At the Royal Gorge in southwestern Wyoming you'll find emerald water. It is a slow-motion landscape. You sleep on a high ridge of land by the water, and it takes an hour for you to watch the flight of a bird, a flight so far down and away from where you are it makes the pony express seem quick. Even though it is hot outside, the water of the Royal Gorge is clear and very cold. It sort of winks at you with security.

Both of these spots, Lake Mead and the Royal Gorge, are hypnotic. You are at the whim of where water doesn't feel right. I suppose they are recreation areas for some, but for me they are contradictions, which, when delirious, I can accept quite well.

The Myth of Big Two Hearted Rivers

My friend from Northern Michigan became a friend because he talked unfair. He talked about the rivers up north, where Hemingway fished. He did this in the winter months of Kansas, when trout fishing couldn't be further away. He could have spoken of the awful winters, the mosquitoes, the singular, repetitive boredom of pine tree after pine tree way up north, but he didn't. He did go on to mention these sort of details later, which made the place seem real again, but he recovered from these details by speaking of wines: cherry, grape, rhubarb. But he mentioned, first, the rivers, and I was caught like a brook trout from then on. I have yet to go to the northern realms of Michigan, up into the northern peninsula, into the land of insects, where the real and imaginary Big Two Hearted rivers flow, but I long to.

This whole northern region interests me much more than the West, where I continually get tricked into exploring time after time. I must quit this and focus on the far reaches of the north country. My friends in the West, who show off their trout waters and rivers, will quiver when I begin inundating them with stories of my "new" fishing waters. I see the places on the map and feel good, the Brule River in Wisconsin for instance. This isn't a competition, but the one thing I always miss about the West is the good trout fishing. It is a bore though. So much praise in a sport that is harmed by praise. Midwestern, northern woods' water is a more apt location for the likes of me (except I have to admit I frequently long for a couple of hidden gems I know of in Idaho). The less showmanship the better the fly fishing. Trout don't like show-offs.

The Body Language of Water

Speak of water and you must stare into space: wide armed gestures will have to get in your way as you describe the girth and finality of the volumes and the movements of liquidy matter, sloshing, slowly, once again rapidly, then flinging in a literal free flow toward the Pacific coast. Crashing without flinching. The Snake river requires gesture.

Or like this. If you are along the banks of the Columbia, and someone pulls up beside you, asks what's the river all about, you will have to look into the distance. You'll have to point with your hands, arms out wide, take a deep breath and say, "This is the Columbia River, it goes all the way to the Pacific, it goes its own way, the way it wants to (pointing)!"

One can use proud body language to explain a river. It is the only honorable way to do so.

THE TRUTH, DAMS AGAIN AND SIMPLICITY

One quality that the river offers, something that you can be more sure of than not sure of, is that a river is true. Whatever it does, it does not lie. It offers something about why people like sporting events so much: they are real and happening, without hiding, right in front of you. There isn't any cue card saying, splash here, riffle here. This alone makes the river unique in this day and age.

A river isn't wrapped up in the momentary shortness of our individual, fleeting, no-matter-what-you-think, soon forgotten (thank goodness) human lives. The river continues, calmly, destined to be real at all moments. That would be a great epitaph for a human, if possible, "Real and true from start to finish." Not one of us is totally true and honest from birth to death, completely. How many of us squeal that we have no interest in the economics of modern society, then turn around and crave a cellular phone, or a fax machine, or a certain bottle of rare wine? How many of us destroy the most valuable aspect of humanity, the soul, by going against human nature, following what turns out to be a short-lived ideological whim?

A dam is a momentary, human bash to the mid-section of a river.

I like to know that, to put it in simple terms, the river will win. Like a rabbit and a tortoise: dams are put up quick, but the constant pressure of the river, beating, whirling, will break through. This is an idea beyond recreational pleasure, beyond energy watts produced, beyond conserving water for drought. It is the original plan for the flow of water.

RIVERS AWAY

Enchantment with bubbles may be the root of all river worship. To feel, to flow. The quest for freedom. To breathe of water. To pop and be born. To stir up our souls and drift. We admire and wish for continuity in lifestyle. To move with ease from urban to rural, from solitude to social. To talk to a rancher as well as to a scholar. The river enters the desert as it does the rain forest, smoothly. If you want to give the river a language, then do so. You will find that it is unpronounceable, yet strong. You will find that the river speaks "river" along its entire journey: language full of comfort, incapable of interpretation. Full of tradition. It moves as it speaks. Over time, given compassion and faith the river begins, but only begins, to make sense.

Listen when you can.

Watch wind ripple water forward while you listen.

TREE TRUNKS

A WORTHY QUESTION MAY BE THIS: WHICH CAME FIRST, THE SYCAMORE TREE OR THE RIVER? I am bound, equally, with them both. I find myself hoping that they were forged, by a lightning bolt and crash of thunder, at the same moment.

I understand that an argument can be made, that without water a tree will perish, lie as bare as a desert landscape, but I would object. First, without a need to water the tree, what value would the river have? Secondly, one may try to live without the other, but when the wind blows, and they aren't together, you can hear, pushed out of the current of a river, or from out the trunk of a tree, a subdued and lonely moaning, as of lovers torn apart. It is haunting to hear the sound. One does not yearn ever to live without the other. They are tangled tightly and snugly. In modern psychological terms, the two have developed a healthy co-dependency.

I sometimes lie awake at night thinking about fly fishing for trout, on a quiet stream lined with sycamore trees. I would not prosper as the blue heron, or the king fisher, but I would be ushered into the feeling of much and many riches. Undoubtedly, I would be in a true and utter netherworld, pending a lack of civilization nearby. The trout would have little to worry about as I would be struck dumb, with strong-felt bliss, for a long and savored period of time without action. Once I began to cast my flies, I'd be influenced, as if on the dope of a higher plane, by the water and the wood.

Polarize your vision. Visualize, or go look at only the mid-sections of a stand of trees, at just the trunks, perhaps of birch or aspen. Notice bright lengths of whitened bark. Look at the trunks some more. There is a worm-like, stream-like meandering you can envision in the lanes of trunk wood. Perhaps you'll see, or hear a splash. It has been rumored that an ancient, at one time nearly extinct, form of life is returning to wild and scenic

74

river banks: the bark trout. With the return of the bark trout, it is believed, by those who believe in this rare, tree fish, that the spotted owl will prosper, as will wolf and bear again. At this time, there is no known fishing lure able to catch this fleeting, well-hidden fish.

My First Venture into Trees

My very first venture into trees and up close to water was around age four. My brother and I went off our yard and into the woods behind our house. We ventured down a slight hill, crawled beneath a large branch, and then walked back up, curving over a slight mound, to a small stand of trees. This long-sounding journey still feels long today, although in reality it was probably no more sixty yards from our backyard fence.

The two of us found tree trunks that had formed from fallen trees, and which were no more than twenty feet from a creek. This was literally a fantasy place. The largest tree trunk was big enough for us to sit in. We called this the King's Throne. There was a long, dead tree trunk, slightly rotted, that we walked on top of to get to the throne, and we called this the King's Trail. We found old pop cans along the creek and rinsed them out, placing them around our throne. Each downed tree was a path to walk on. Feeling good in the woods, by water, was easy for me right away. I have always enjoyed this.

Treehouses

Three storied, and standing year after year as a snack shop, the treehouse was built up from the base of a pear tree. It's one of the easiest memories I have of a tree being part of my life. I don't know who laid the first board, I don't even know where we got the wood to make a three storied treehouse, but we did. There was an article in the local paper about the thing, entitled Candy Land. From this treehouse my friends and I progressed to forts built along the creek.

These forts were of wood. We would take fork sticks, a rare piece of wood that we would search long and hard to locate. The fork stick could be used as a corner support and was the first step to a good structure. The only thing better than a good fork stick was a triple-forked stick. Then, with branches, which there was an abundance of, since the Dutch Elm Disease[25] had laid half the trees to rest in our woods, we would continue by making the walls. Finally, we would roof and finish off the walls of the forts with bark chunks, massive overlapping strips of bark that easily kept out the rain. There is no question that the building of these forts along the creek was one the most important activities of my childhood.

We went on to make snow-packed sledding ramps, pulleys that we rode across ravines, road bikes, skateboarded, played school sports; but I would say that nothing was as interesting as making forts. This is where I was wed to wood.

---

[25] This Dutch Elm Disease was actually quite a traumatic moment in my life. My parents hired someone to cut down all the sick trees, and the woods behind us vanished. I never understood why we were the only ones to do this. No one else hired tree cutters. Right behind our house was the only real bare spot. It is also strange that the whole epidemic wasn't explained. Such things really ought to be.

Restoration and a Word from My Grandfather

Wood symbolizes care and maintenance. It is unlike the joys of river life for me. I feel as if wood is something to be taken quite, very, seriously.[26] A river, left to its natural course of things, seems more likely to sustain itself.

Items built with wood, unless preserved, will lose (at least change) some of their shape and quality. I admire and look with wonder at restored wood floors. A well laid and maintained wood floor is a thing of beauty because of the care that is being displayed.

Wood floors are over-exaggerated, however. I think people admire them for their pristine appearance. It is infinitely warmer, on a cold winter day, to have carpet and plywood underboarding. A friend of mine explained the wide planked Cherry wood floor he had up in Northern Michigan. He went on about them. The verdict was, "It was damn hard to keep the place warm, with wind whipping in between the boards during the winter, but they were tremendously awesome to walk on and see."

I had wood flooring, above a crawl space, in Kansas. One of the room's floor boards contracted quite a bit (I believe this may be due to not using enough nails when laying the boards, as much as to the weather), but another room hardly at all. Laying, sanding, uncovering all the things that go into creating a wood floor in a house are

---

[26] An old friend of mine, perhaps wise, I am not certain yet, said an interesting thing once: he said that a person enjoys classical music with a frown. I think this is right and like wood for me, a serious enjoyment. Like grinning at the moment I am able to split a chunk of osage orange for firewood. Smiling for the hard work. I believe that wood inhabits the realm of good work.

well worth the effort. I would have no other style of flooring: the hassles don't exceed the value.

Another interesting aspect of wood: still to be frowned at, but immensely enjoyed, are the surprises of restoring older homes from what I should call the "wood era" of building. Not houses made of pressboard and flimsy 2 x 4's. Let me call it, more aptly, the age of hand cut wood when each board wasn't identical, but each board was strong. These days, it seems that 2 x 4's are getting regularly smaller and smaller as time goes by. Soon the measurements will probably be 1.89 x 2.88, but of course still be called 2 x 4's. I can see it now. Someday, in a hollywood-like scene: I'll be standing along a trout stream, talking to a youngster. Telling how, back in my days, they used wood for building and that those things you see now, those plastic strips being used for building houses, are based upon wooden boards we used to measure in inches. We'd called them 2 x 4's.

Another friend of mine, who regularly surprises me with his mastery knowledge of wood, lives in Madison, Indiana, a town that he describes as rich in 19th century, Midwestern architecture. While working on his house, removing some crappy mid-20th century siding, he discovered long, original boards. Wood as long as the portion of the house he was uncovering. This became a moment when he went berserk with joy. I can imagine it like this: a good and serious, at-work look, turned into wonder, reflection, rechecking, pondering, then amazement, culminating with a wail of splendor.

Another surprise, vital to wood, had to do with an incident in my old house, built in 1890. I had exposed

78

the original ceiling rafters, when I saw that the boards were each a unique size, displaying hand-hewn marks along their sides. Also, while trying to momentarily hang an electric wire from nails in these rafters, I bent five roofing nails, then broke a drill bit trying to do so. Aged strength is a factor you don't anticipate. You can't plan for it. A house is not built with this prediction in mind. However, it would be interesting to build and sell houses like wine: house built and aged ten years, 50 years, 100 years. You could talk like this, "1859, a very good year for houses located in the Wisconsin River watershed region, having been a mildly humid summer and being built with local, native Oak...."[27]

I could go on and on about surprises in old wood and acts of restoring, but I'll suffice by saying that working with wood is truly good. I am blessed with this type of work as well. My grandfather, whom I have had many years to reflect upon since he passed away years ago, was the one person who seemed to take the most time in understanding who I was in my family. He told me, one summer, when I was young, that I was good at using a hammer and saw. I take pride in this. It is the only observance, of my skills, ever told to me early in my life by a relative. I think of it often. Perhaps this is why I am drawn to wood and the labor of restoration. It reminds me of who I am, or of whom I want to become.

---

[27] The human impulse to build with wood is so strong that we have nearly scraped the planet of all old growth trees. This is similar to trying to block the flow of all our rivers with dams, trying to make lakes. It seems hard for humans to recognize that something good is only good until over done.

Osage Orange

No talk of the species tree, and its offspring wood, can go without mentioning strength. Nothing could be as strong as the hammer of Thor, except perhaps one type of wood I know about: Osage Orange, the thing we Plainsmen call Iron Wood, the rugged, bright yellow wood with a heat index, when burned, that puts Hickory to shame. The wood that blunts, strips, and laughs at the blades of a table saw. Some call it hedgewood, but no one I know is brave enough to make fun of it. You would make fun of the Osage Orange tree only if you wanted to die hard, and wished to carry extra bad luck until your hard death occurred. Have you ever seen the stuff polished, formed, milled, made into a picture frame? I promise that when you do, you'll have to hold your breath in amazement.

I have spent many, many, many hours splitting, with an ax, the cordwood of Osage Orange. I used to make my neighbor dumbfounded. He would walk over, laugh, and say, "Man, I can't believe you're my neighbor. I live next to a fool." Being a finishing carpenter and architect, he knew a certain amount about what he spoke of. I would use saws, wedges, hammers and of course an ax, splitting almost nothing for hours. Freezing at first, but slowly, the heat index of the stuff would heat me by chopping. I chipped and broke many axes, but still, I chopped on. Clanging, bashing, enjoying every second. Sure I loved the challenge, but even more so, I wanted the intimacy of being with the wood. To be working into it, with it, pulling the sappy, bright yellow stuff apart is exhilarating. It is a slow process well worth doing. I intend to chip and break many more axes on the stuff.

IT STANDS ALONE

There are people who record and study the continuity of society and nature. They gather knowledge of traditions, make use of formal education, and decipher various patterns to state conclusions based upon hypothesis. These people amaze me with their belief (or presumption) that they have actually figured something out.[28]

These people are often the same ones who can "follow the directions," when assembling something. Is there a similarity between those who, "read the directions," and the varied patterns and rings that symbolize the growth of trees to people? I don't think so.

Some trees live in the dense forest of the Pacific Northwest. In regions way up north, such as Minnesota and Michigan, a tree in a forest learns to live as others, forming straight up, and more slowly out, searching for sun, in the proximity allowed by others. Some may be dwarfed for years, waiting for the grand, large Cottonwood or Pine to teeter, and bring to an end a living education, while at the same time allowing an opening in which to grow in. While dwarfed a tree can surely work on good roots and inventive manners of

---

[28] Formal study has always spooked me for this reason. People attempt to "learn" what they already believe. Rarely do humans begin a futile task. The results seem less an act of knowledge as an act of justification based upon initial belief, merely exercises in confirmation, and not, then, really learning at all. Most of the time this demands a closed mind, aimed at guarded conclusions; then mocking and irritation when asked questions which require feeling and thinking beyond the proposed, or predestined "conclusions."

survival. (I've often laughed at a joke I made up one day, walking around somewhere in northern Idaho. That if you could hear the little tree speaking to the big one you might hear this: "When I get older, Uncle Sugar Pine, I hope to grow up.") The creative trees may be those that grow at angles, twist and have odd-shaped, oversized limbs. Their desire for life is strong. One, even in a crowd, need not be fully controlled by others.

Then there is the sole, isolated tree, silhouetted in the sunset, casting a super long shadow across miles of grass. It is gnarled, unique and one of kind, also ingenious and creative. Directions, as such, are not relevant in this case of growth, because, alone, life must be figured out, as other giants must do, in an entire region where only they can exist. In these cases it's better to be aware of the beauty in tradition, and learn, more or less, by accident and hard effort about how to live.

A tree can be a good, although vague, teacher in these matters of creative independence. The isolated tree, standing in farm fields or along a border between plains and forest, is a Master. In the Badlands there is a tree— half dead, half alive—which stands like a gate to the dry, riveting hills that I admire each trip I take there. Sometimes, to impress myself, I stand in the middle of an area in the Badlands, or other places, at sunset and see how long and wide a shadow I can cast, as if a lone tree, trying to gain the feeling of permanence.

I have, from time to time, rushed to the dense growth and cover of the pine forest, to feel part of the group. Always I leave though. I can not live with direction in the form of one plus one. I need to struggle as a lone prairie tree, dodging lightning bolts, as I stand in place. When I read or hear directions I comprehend one out of every six words. I regularly absorb the effects of a broken limb (to myself) due to stupidity, selective bad hearing and stubbornness. I realize that I am untrained and, knowingly, untrainable. I need space to make mistakes in and need to grow as a tree, alone, casting my own shadow. It is not wrong to live as a tree. I recommend everyone choose a tree and imitate it, literally.

ROCKS, AND THE POSSIBILITIES OF BECOMING A TREE: A LEGEND
One big rock sits atop a hill and is chipped apart slowly by the wind. This one big rock was pushed across the earth with the glaciers and marks the edge of the final glacial period. Then, one large crack on this rock began to form. Something it never thought possible of itself in younger years before.

Next, when the rains came in the fall, the winter followed and frozen water in the crack split off a big chunk of stone that fell to the ground, chipping lightly as it tumbled, landing, half in-half out, of a creek.

Over time, as the water gushed over this stone along the creek, more cracks opened up, these cracks broadened, but no more chips fell off. What began to emerge were the roots of a tree. These roots had started deep inside the rock, back when dirt had been rolled in to the Big Rock as it was shoved by a glacier during the Ice Age. Now this ancient dirt, having mixed with rock, was growing out of the stone and into the ground. Each spring the roots awaited the increased flow of water down the creek, rich and high water; which would help establish endurance to make it through the last part of the summer, on into early fall, when the creek would briefly be completely dry.

Over time, from inside the chip of stone and the roots that were taking hold, emerged a large and stable Willow tree, long and flowing branches, in tribute to the creek and roots made from out of the rock. One after another the one Big Rock up on the hilltop fell to pieces and slowly other trees emerged: Cottonwoods, Silver Maples, Mulberries, and even a few Walnuts. The banks of the creek ought to have been called the Rock Forest, but who could have known this is how trees and rocks play together?

Now, when you hear the saying: each large boulder contains a forest, each small stone a tree and each grain of sand a leaf that's fallen, you will understand.

FIREFLY HATCH

Late at night, to the tune of crickets and locusts you can see the dance of the earth stars. Given enough day time heat and a sufficient agreement between the other insects, the fireflies will come out and play, pretending to be the stars and will dance amongst the high leaves of the trees, who act as hosts. If one looks up, in a dark meadow at night, the flicks of light are mesmerizing. During the day the fireflies live in the tips of the trees, absorbing the light they will release at night. Then, come around midnight, with a light breeze, the leaves stir, opening the "show" like curtains. The blinking fireflies keep up until morning or until the weather gets too cold for the crickets to perform with them. All of this occurs in isolation. It is not a given. It is an extra benefit, one might say, to exploring the realms of being alive. One must sneak up slowly, not disturbing anything to see the performance. One hint: it is wise to hold your applause until later the next day, when the fireflies are asleep.

SHADE

In the way of the sun's journey to the earth stands the tree. Between the tree and the ground rests shade. Can you live without a shadow? No. A tree takes pride in this work. It maintains and works in its own environment, creating the shade needed by its forefathers: the roots. The tree's shade invites worms to its side by maintaining workable, moist earth. Birds and animals provide other, needed nutrients and live in direct relationship to the tree's ability to create a safe and livable environment. A tree without a bird or squirrel nest is suspect, perhaps not fully healthy.

Self-creating protection from the elements—sun, drought and wind—is an ability. A tree learns to adapt and grow in its specific location. If not, it perishes. Simple.

A tree must be native to its land to prosper. As the last lines of Wendell Berry's poem, "The Sycamore," go: *"I see that it stands in its place, and feeds upon it, and is fed upon, and is native, and maker."*[29]

---

[29] From Wendell Berry's *Collected Poems* (North Point Press 1985 ed. page 65). A true gem of a poem.

85

As is the structure of a tree, so is a family tree based upon sturdy branches that are to hold the family together. As there is, for some traditions, a coat of arms, most likely there is a family wood as well, which started the tradition of drawing out the family tree. This family wood was used to exemplify the family tree.

Visualize this. When a child is born, the family plants a tree in the child's honor. With each family member's tree in a grove you have the family as trees, branching in heights and successes from out of the ground.

Or take the family cemetery, circled by the eternal life of the conifer tree. This seems another form of the family tree. Although the conifer is one particular strain of wood, it surrounds and binds the larger idea of a family well, making the whole cemetery one family, everlasting.

Why do we think of our families as trees? It can't simply be because of a similarity between branching out and limbs. Many things fan and spread out: a splash in the water spreads out, ant beds branch and spread.... The base of a tree is an immovable, lasting item, the family name. Yet a single tree doesn't last as potentially long as a "family tree." I believe it is along the same lines as my belief that wood and trees are serious items of pleasure. In this way, a family is to be taken seriously, and what better to symbolize this than with a tree, a form of life that continually adapts and learns to grow.

TREE AS SACRED

One can venture through spiritual thought and find mention of the tree and wood. Gautama Buddha returned numerous times as a tree, and the bo-tree is part of Buddhist tradition. One will probably have heard many times of the tree of life. Why wouldn't a tree be sacred? Most trees, even short-lived ones, the poplar for instance, can last a good portion, if not longer than a single human's life. Humans can really only judge mortality from out of themselves, thus, a thing lasting longer than a person contains the potential for immortality. You may pay homage to a tree that your grandfather planted, or spoke of, in his life. This makes the tree a very sacred object of living history. An object passed on which is visible and alive, serves powerfully for aspects of oral tradition. An enormous tree trunk known by a great-grandfather can be mesmerizing, an object cherished for many generations. It is powerful to worship the same object as a great-grandfather did.

If one considers the pine tree, the thought of eternal life is inevitable. If one thinks of totem poles, then the thought of wood as the base for pride is strong.

The tree as serious is quite evident in the Garden of Eden. The fruit of the tree is thought of as man's demise from innocence. In nearly all belief systems there is a mention and involvement of the tree.

DIVINING ROD, DOWSING

Although one can use the act of dowsing to find many things—treasure, coal, iron, or other useful items—the image one is most accustomed to is dowsing for water.

One can also use many objects to dowse with, a metal rod, a fiberglass strip, but the most common item thought of, and used, is the forked piece of hazelwood. There is no better marriage between wood, humans, and water than dowsing.

The reality of being able to sense water by the uncontrollable movement of a stick is extraordinary, yet it is also something real. I know people who have relatives that can use a divining rod quite proficiently. Place a piece of wood in their hands, above a spot they have divined, and they will get to shaking. I have heard it said that "diviners" have a rather different body charge. When they wear watches on their wrist, the watch stops. If they sit by a clock in a living room, the clock will slowly begin to go backwards. Maybe they are people of the Southern Hemisphere, captive in the Northern.

Metabolism churning away counterclockwise, sensing water backwards, felt before visible, tasted before drunk. Dowsers could easily be part tree. It would make sense—a tree must search and find water, it's a matter of life and death.

OCEAN TREES

Angled in opposition or relaxing along with the constant stream of shoreline wind, is the coastal tree. This tree is a strange breed—a twisting and angular growth. They look like arrowheads from one angle. Their form, which looks paused (caught in a constant breeze, or tensed up in anticipation of the next wave), can remind one of many things. One is the painful manner in which some cultures form the human body: binding the feet to stay small or placing necklaces around the neck, pushing down the collar bone and chest for the sake of appearance.

Like a good sports car, the aerodynamics of a coastal pine also come to mind. A smooth angular transition toward the mainland. Half tree, half branch. What it may be saying is this, "Follow the green side of the tree to the garden and the depths of the forest."

A coastal pine must live with indecision. The temptation of the lush, full, dense forest is behind it, always inviting, until you feel suffocated. Then you must leave and follow back to the other side of the ocean pine, the bare and open side down to the sandy beach.

Walking Sticks

Most people like the idea of a walking stick. They don't really know how to merge walking with a stick, but instead just like gripping a stick of wood in their hands. I am sure there are countless numbers of sticks that get tossed into vans and cars, which get set aside in carports, which collect spider webs, then get broken and perhaps burned months later as fire kindling, or found, years later, when cleaning out the garage.

The attractions of the walking stick seem to be a need to feel busy and part of the surroundings, combining wood with skin. Perhaps, while walking along with a walking stick in hand, you'll day dream of the need to use the walking stick to fend off angry animals or "unruly" people. Walking sticks can also help when looking for something, or can become an item to demonstrate who you think you are. Surely, if you've looked for a stick, you know that not any stick will do.

Some people enjoy and like walking sticks more than for the sake of having one while in the woods. They like the process of making, or rather "perfecting," a piece of wood into a stick of their own. This is an appreciation of wood and woodwork. These people often understand how to use a walking stick: for assistance, balance, and scavenging. A good walking stick can be immensely helpful while looking for morel mushrooms, for instance.

Totem Poles

Secluded and obvious all at once. A hidden tree. A hidden totem pole. I always imagine that a totem pole, in the right region, the Pacific Northwest and British Columbia, would sneak up on me. That I would be looking and then, KABOOM, I would see it there in front of me, lurking. Perhaps it would have crept up on me.

What process goes into picking the tree that will be used for the totem? It is probably like picking a walking stick, but intensified. Surely, the carvings and the meanings aren't just carved on any shape, or type of wood. One is reminded, in a non-branching manner, of the family tree theory. I would be curious if the lack of branching (if my idea of a totem pole as a family symbol is even remotely correct) is a belief in a more linear family system, than a branching family. Perhaps the totem pole is a coniferous tradition resulting from the lack of broad branching trees. Even if there is no shortage of diverse branching trees, then maybe conifers are used because they require ingenuity to set them apart from each other.

BARNS

My father-in-law out West and I are obsessed with barns.
I don't really know why. We gawk at wooden, massive
barns. Metal outbuildings don't interest us. He has
purchased and used the materials of at least three barns
that I know of and speaks of building barns all the time.
I look forward, with much longing, to helping him build
a barn someday. This is one event in my life I want to be
a part of. It will be an initiation rite in some way, or an
act of equal importance to an initiation when this finally
happens.

I long to live in a barn, to find a good, old, big barn
and turn it into a house, with lofts and high ceilings.[30]
Please don't talk about common sense around me when
I think this, though. Common sense will put you in a
small, pressboard, stick-and-plywood dwelling.

When my father-in-law and I are together, driving
to a river, you can guess what the conversation is like
between us, driving by barns. "Now that's a good barn,"
or, "Did you see that barn?!" or "Did I tell you about my
plans to build a barn of cordwood, with timber framing
and a free standing masonry fireplace with solar panels
and that I found an old barn and bought the wood to
start it all with...?" I believe, that if either of us ever
mentioned something to do with barns and the need for
metal (except nails, although a pegged barn is desirable),
that would be the end of something good. We'd have to
stop talking for life.

---

[30] I have come to the conclusion that old, thick timbered barns are cathedrals.
They are big enough that you can't know everything in them, like a great
church, at once. Yet a barn is trusted interior space. The space in a barn
stands out of time.

On a good day, wooden barns are us. They carry us away into fantastic possibilities. They are interior, yet outdoor, space. On a bad day, one of us says he's moving away, or has no money to be part of traveling to the barn raising, putting the shared, "barn thing" temporarily out of reach for a while.

I'll never forget when he bought his first barn. Three hundred dollars, I think, for the whole thing. When he told me he'd bought it we both couldn't believe it. We stood by the massive structure and chicken hopped, or did some strange expression of amazement. "Holy crap! This whole thing is yours? Wow!" I kept thinking and saying. We pulled large planks around for hours and generally goofed off with the large quantity of wood now available to us.

We returned after the purchase, unable to talk, jittery and amazed, to his cabin nearby. We talked, but were kind of in another world of thought. We put a roof on his cabin in a lightning storm during the afternoon, not really aware of the lightning until we thought about going fishing.

FLOW THROUGH GIANT REDWOODS, OR PLANTAE CELEREIUS REDWOOD
Right near the coast of the Pacific, everyone knows that if you travel through northern California you will edge along and through the redwoods. Perhaps the most massive trunks of wisdom we have available to us. (I've never quite understood why the cut-down trees are occasionally put on display other than to verify stupidity.)

Noise is mystified in the redwoods, along with proportions. So that to wade creeks and to think of water is altered. Height seems absurd in a grove of redwoods. Then, after a while, you forget their height because what suddenly sinks into your brain is the pure girth of the trunks at your eye level. This happens since you really can't take in a whole redwood at once. Your mind works hard to break them down into understandable items but can't.

One of the first things I think of when standing in a creek, or stream, next to redwoods is the amount of water that a redwood must go through every day. I believe an average redwood tree, say, two-hundred to two-hundred fifty feet, must need countless gallons of water to maintain, even more to grow. You would think that you could hear the sucking of water standing in a grove of trees. I have tried to hear this noise, and put my ears to the trunks. I don't know what I've heard, but since there is most definitely a distinct sound in the redwoods, a type of hollow and subdued silence, this must be the river of water, creeping up the trunks.

Such girth is overwhelming. To stand beside a redwood is truly dwarfing; your perception is abused. You try to spread your arms, puff up your chest, look as big as possible, and you look even smaller for your attempt. You stand in the trees and feel their height. You walk out of the immensity of these things, a little away, into an opening by a creek and you're left wondering, is the creek beside me really this small, or are the trees so big?

The manner in which the trunks of the redwood spew from the ground, with such abruptness, reminds me of stalks of celery. Straight and narrow. Grainy. The way celery will pull water through it must be like that of a redwood. Perhaps, although it may seem strange, a redwood tree is part of the celery family, a vegetable and not a wood at all. It is prehistoric food for early herbivore life forms.

FOOD BEARING TREES

Nuts and fruit. Miracles really. To care for a plant, get shade and be rewarded with fruit is amazing. I believe that everyone should have at least one food-bearing tree since these trees take sympathy and care to be cultivated well. A wormy apple possesses a misunderstood upbringing. Taking care of a fruit tree ought to be part of a training program for parenthood. It is a manifestation of concern, yet redeemable through consumption. It would be good to know how to reward oneself with homegrown peach, or apple pie. Possibly even cherry wine.

BARK

Inside the top coat lies the truth. The bark is part tree, part bug, part air, part armor. A shield. We could think of it as clothing. It keeps trees protected until they're ready to be exposed. The reasons differ from tree to tree, but like skin and clothing, bark is helpful. Like people, as they grow older, they take on the look of dignity. The bark of a tree is worth studying closely. It is the finger print of its existence.

Some people are weekend warriors or city workers with
nothing better to do than prune, and in the process hack
away at trees until, after mutilation and mutilation, they
have destroyed the tree. You will see a cleared yard in
the forest, for no reason other than unrestrained clear
cutting. Money is probably involved, but also, the feeling
of power, such as that of people who carry guns in their
trucks, in populated areas. People love to clear and cut
and putter around and a lot of the time, trees (and all of
wildlife) take a beating. These same people may go to a
nursery and get replacement trees, something they can
look forward to hacking at later.

Thinking of trees as a renewable crop is technically
true, and this has a place in the timber industry, but not
in folks' backyards or vacant lots. It is sad that it is
considered out-of-the-ordinary to save the trees when
building something, and not common.

Hacker meets saver. My friend from California has
a second home in Oregon. He hired a backhoe operator
to help put in a septic system and the guy told me, to the
side, "These people from California can't stand to cut
down a tree. It's not like we don't have any trees around
here." It was a hassle to dig trenches for the septic and
the electric line without knocking down some trees, but
it was possible and really, much preferred. The hacker
lives a truly utilitarian and momentary, non-visual life I
believe. He (or she) doesn't sense the country coated
with trees, the beauty of green and the value of life
presented in a thick stand of Aspens. However, the saver
can get carried away. No single tree, when building a

house, is absolutely worthy of not being cut down. Granted, as long as this theory of the single tree doesn't get carried away. Individual life forms are not, philosophically speaking, completely and fully valuable. This goes for trees as well as humans. Any extreme is harmful.

A synthesis is the oasis. I venture that both hacker and saver would agree, an oasis is a place that is physically and mentally beautiful. An oasis is not the same for everyone. In Kansas, some people think Colorado is just too damn hilly and covered with too many trees. Some people in Iowa think Chicago is too packed with cement.... The image of the palm tree oasis has formed because it is a balance: water and green growth in the dry and sandy desert. The oasis is a confirmation for this reason, and why the hacker and saver can agree: it is a balance and not an extreme. Just enough cleared, just enough standing. A place where everyone has what they want. In their own life, people should strive to make trees part of a balance to create a natural oasis for themselves and other life forms as well.

Water Becomes Wood and Wood Becomes Water

Float inside the growth of wood grain, flow down stream, lathered in moving current. I have always been captivated by rivers and trees. I can't imagine life without them. In many ways the two are one.

Great Blue Herons, Rivers and Sycamore Trees: Synthesis Number 1

In my opinion no talk of rivers and trees would be complete without a full and lengthy discussion of great blue herons, water, and sycamore trees. Together, as if a recipe, they are the ingredients that make rivers. Stir well tiny chunks of sycamore bark with the stare of twenty blue herons, then let rise until you hear the herons bark loud enough to be the sound of the moon rising. Soon this mixture will create water, which, with the flaps of heron wings, will begin to flow toward a larger body of water. As the sycamore tree grows, as many as three to four hundred years, it both protects and becomes part of nearby water. Each year the blue herons, which gave birth to the water, will return and sit in their nests, or rather, thrones, and provide part of the spring floods.

As I said, without fail, ask me to think about a river, or tree, and after thirty seconds I will conjure up the image of a blue heron. Either one standing motionless, one flying away, one barking, or one landing, far less gently than you might imagine, in a tree.

From creeks on the Konza Prairie to gushing currents in the Pacific Northwest, blue herons are there, making certain the rivers are flowing. I have never seen a heron land on a dam. This is because they detest them. They send scouts, ravens, to muster together armies to destroy these things that are blocking their invention: the river.

Herons emit shadows that even the sun can't cast. Their silence, before barking, is as intense as their eyesight. When they fly you can feel the air vibrate. It's what a giant heavyweight boxer might do if he could punch the air and knock it out.

I don't see any reason not to say that the heron is the synthesis of wood mixed with water. One needs more synthesis in this day and age of duality: two-party politics; yes-and-no morality; good and bad luck, black and white, digital electronics. At some point questions have to arise: where are all the pairs headed, what are their results? Is everything an opposite of each other? Synthesis is necessary, but also hard work. Synthesis, when put in terms of thought and action should be considered similar to something Karl Marx wrote, *"The philosophers have only interpreted the world, in various ways; the point, however, is to change it."* [31]

Another way to appreciate the need for synthesis is the meaning of the small phrase, *Standing by Words*, also the title for an essay by Wendell Berry.[32] The point being that words and actions must have a strong relationship to be useful. What is said must be understood and accomplished.

Consider, then, that when sitting in a tree, amongst a nest of sticks, the heron looks like a small sycamore branch.[33] Consider that a heron in the sky, flying,

---

[31] This quote is from Part XI of Marx's *Theses on Feuerbach*. In this regard the philosophy of Praxis is useful. One must move from the ideal, to the real, to action. A good source for understanding these ideas is available by Shlomo Avineri, *The Social and Political Thought of Karl Marx* (Cambridge Press, 1968).

[32] "Standing by Words," from *Standing by Words* (North Point Press, 1983). This essay does a terrific job of pointing out the need to work on the process of synthesis.

[33] Actually, it crossed my mind that a heron can hide in a sycamore tree, its body long, with a simple sharp curve to its head. Sitting in a curly, burly, wound up oak tree a blue heron would be spotted right away.

appears, in some ways, to be a flying piece of wood. Consider that herons, when hunting, spend almost all their time in the water and that they are dependent on what water, and rivers can provide them. Consider that sycamore trees are a heron's favorite nesting habitiat, or rather rookery. Consider that sycamore trees grow primarily along streams. Consider that a heron can stand in a river and leave no ripples. Consider that a heron's feet rarely touch anything but wood and water. Consider that without each, wood and water, the heron would be incomplete.

The heron is a portable container of water, cured and seasoned by rainstorms, mist, fog, mud, and sap. Their eggs are hatched near moving water and the first noise a new born heron may hear is wind blowing over water, wood, and leaves. The first flight the new born takes will be to water. I have dreamt that a great blue heron's eggs are simply containers of river water that are sucked up through the roots of sycamore trees. A process that starts when the brown seed balls of the sycamore tree hit the ground in autumn.

It is unquestionable that the great blue heron is a tribute, and product of both wood and water.

SYNTHESIS NUMBER 2

I don't see any reason not to say that a sycamore tree isn't the super slow motion of a river. If you slow down a river, make one particular spot of river take three-hundred years to move as far as a sycamore tree has grown in the same period of time, lay this portion of the river upright, it seems certain that you'd see the branches and white patches of the sycamore tree.

THEY BECOME AS ONE

The river turns to tree turns to water to river: the shapeshifter theory is resurrected. Nature learns to grow together, to alternate, separate and be as one. The river that floats above the ground in Nebraska and the River Without Water in South Dakota were once ocean waves, which were once waters raised from the depths of the earth, out of a spring creek that emerged through the roots of a sycamore grove in an isolated backyard in Indiana.

Such places as these, where birds and trees and rivers are born, co-exist, mingle, and blink on and off. Shimmer to form mirages. These places exist because they are only partly true, yet more true than false and where, from time to time, things become real.

The rivers and the trees must exist, as the wolf must, as the grizzly must, as the uninterrupted flow of clean water must. These realms of water and wood appear in the human mind because they are linked with necessity and dreams. To go without the river and the trunks of trees would be to live in a cardboard box, eating microwave dinners. It would be to have newsprint ink scuffed all over your hands and face. It would be all the most unnatural things. It would be to feel permanently homeless. Unrooted.

It is good to remember, as you walk along a riverbank lined with trees that the human body is mostly made of water. You don't need to be a Zen master to call yourself a river, or a tree. See what becomes of this: merge into wood by sticking out your arms to the sun, envision that your toes are searching for water alongside the banks of a river. Let this feeling last.

The text of this book was set in Adobe Garamond. The
Garamond typeface was designed by Jean Jannon in 1615.
Garamond is characterized by little contrast between the thick and
thin letter strokes, heavily bracketed serifs, and oblique stress.
The letterforms are open and round, making the face
extremely readable.

This book was printed on 62#, acid free, recycled,
natural halopaque paper.

Printing by Gilliland Printing, Inc.,
Arkansas City, Kansas

Book design by Andy Driscoll and John Patzman

Cover design and typesetting by John Patzman

Cover painting and printer's device created by Andy Driscoll

Ice Cube Press Publication Notes

Additional copies of *River Tips and Tree Trunks* may be obtained for
$14.95 each, plus $1.75 shipping (orders over five, ask about
discounts).

Subscriptions to *Sycamore Roots*, the Ice Cube Press' quarterly journal,
are available for $8.00 per year. *Sycamore Roots* comments on issues
of nature and community—offering creative intuitions on
construction, landscape, gardening, and regionalist thought.

Send inquiries and orders to:

The Ice Cube Press
205 North Front Street
North Liberty, Iowa 52317-9302

Please include payment (check or money order) with purchase
requests. Remember to include your name and complete address
with your order. Expect 2-3 weeks delivery.